WEAVING THE WINDS,
Emily Howell Warner

by
Ann Lewis Cooper

Emily Howell Warner in United Air Lines' CAE Simulator, 2002

1ˢᵗ Books Library™
Bloomington, Indiana

ISBN: 1-4107-5447-2 (e-book)
ISBN: 1-4107-5446-4 (Paperback)
ISBN: 1-4107-5445-6 (Dust Jacket)

Library of Congress Control Number: 2003093051

This book is printed on acid free paper.

Printed in the United States of America
Bloomington, IN

Warner, Emily Howell.
Weaving the Winds, Emily Howell Warner;
by Ann Lewis Cooper. – 1st ed.

1. Warner Emily Howell   2. Aviation – United States – Biography
3. Women air pilots – United States – Biography.
4. Women's Issues—Unites States

I. Cooper, Ann Lewis   II. Title

1stBooks - rev. 07/02/03

TABLE OF CONTENTS

A First Frontier for a Woman
6 February 1973

Best Wishes Carolyn
Emily Warner

FOREWORD: THERE IS SOMETHING SPECIAL ABOUT EMILY

by Billy Walker, Captain, Frontier Airlines and America West

I first met Emily Hanrahan Howell Warner in 1958 when she was a teenager. I was learning basics from Jim Muncey, the Chief Flight Instructor at Clinton Aviation, a well-known and respected flight school operating out of Stapleton International Airport, Denver, Colorado. Emily Hanrahan, one of Jim Muncey's flight students, was working as a receptionist for Clinton Aviation.

There is something special about Emily. All who met her discovered a determined young woman. Eventually, the rest of the world would discover that she was unstoppable. When she became this country's first female airline pilot in the modern, jet-equipped fleet, she opened a door that had been locked to U.S. women for seventy years following the 1903 Wright Brothers' first powered flight.

Many U.S. women had become pilots. My own mother, Frances Emily Nesbitt Walker, was the first female to learn to fly in Wyoming in the 1930s. Several women learned to fly before and after WWI and, during WWII, over 1,000 Women Airforce Service Pilots (WASP) flew everything from the single-engine Piper to the P-51 Mustang, a fighter, and the B-29 bomber.

Much bias and resistance to such a radical interference to one of the male bastions existed and remained in existence when Emily invaded the male dominated cockpits at Frontier. There were sniggering references to women drivers in U.S. airlines' offices and several old hands at Frontier had strong views of womanhood. Some felt women belonged in the kitchen, barefoot and pregnant. Many times Emily was faced with flying in a flight deck filled with tension. No person could have handled being first better than Emily. Soon, she had most of those bigoted pilots, admittedly few in number, amazed at her ability and professionalism. Disdain quickly changed to admiration.

Flying lessons led to possibilities that far exceeded Emily's expectations. They became the pathway to her own career and Emily made it possible for hundreds of women pilot aspirants to follow. The number grows daily. As I write this, at America West, where I am a pilot-instructor, there are more than 30 female pilots.

But it was no mean feat. Emily was filled with the enthusiasm of youth. Little did she know that she would have to experience hard work and frustration for more than 15 years and 7,000 flying hours before her efforts would be taken seriously. Emily's quest to fly was dogged and resolute.

Every step Emily took made history. 29 January 1973 was Emily's new hire class date. Soon she took the "Third Man" seat [a Second Officer, or Flight Engineer position] on the Boeing 737 when, on 6 February 1973, she flew with the venerable Captain Swede Nettleblad and First Officer Glen Tidwell. Her first flight as co-pilot [First Officer] was on 1 August 1974 in the DHC-6 Twin Otter. The date stayed with me because I was in the left seat. We often flew together, sharing the flight deck in the Otter and the Convair 580. She performed her duties very professionally. In a word, she was excellent.

Between 1973 and Frontier's demise in 1986, Emily flew as First Officer and Captain on the de Havilland DHC-6, Convair 580, and Boeing 737. In 1986, she commanded the first all female flight crew. Following the demise of Frontier, Emily spent two years flying the Boeing 737 with Continental. From 1988 to 1990 she flew as a Boeing 727 captain with United Parcel Service before accepting employment with the Federal Aviation Agency as an Aviation Safety Inspector. Having amassed well over 21,000 flight hours, she has served as an Aircrew Program Manager assigned to United Air Lines Boeing 737 fleet.

Emily has been honored nationally and internationally. In demand as a speaker, Emily's message is for young and old, male and female: determination and persistence are the vital traits that help anyone to succeed. Time has proven that she was an excellent choice to pioneer women into the U.S. airliner flight deck.

Atta boy, Girl!

CHAPTER 1: IN PERSPECTIVE, PARALLELS CONVERGE

Emily Hanrahan was born in 1939 in Denver, Colorado. Her Irish American heritage gave her spunk, the poverty of her early years gave her ambition, and coming of age in the United States of the 1950s and 1960s gave her opportunities. The fact that she was female placed hurdles in her path, but Emily was never the kind of woman to let a few obstacles slow her down. The changes wrought by the tumultuous period known as "The Sixties" benefited a woman like Emily, even when she eschewed the legal routes that could have forced her hand.

What was Emily's world like? Who was she and how did she turn obstacles into stepping stones, skepticism into acceptance and, ultimately, admiration?

As a drawing leads to a portrait, we will follow the career of Emily Warner and learn to know her. We will discover the remarkable woman within. *Drawing by Konrad Hack, ASAA*

Prelude to "The Sixties," more a cultural era than a decade

In the United States, the deep roots of the Sixties didn't flower overnight. They tapped the social policies of Franklin Delano Roosevelt's New Deal that first saw light in the 1930s, blossomed with vast governmental programs for public works, and flourished during the 1950s. In an effort to overcome the devastation of the Great Depression of the 1930s, Roosevelt established far-reaching economic and political policies, yet some that also raised the specter of creeping socialism. His New Deal, increasing government involvement in the lives of U.S. citizens, was interrupted with the onslaught of World War II; the 1940s plunged the U.S. into a headlong rush to defeat identifiable enemies in Europe and in Asia.

Although posters decry and the sane agree that "War Is Hell," war economically revitalizes an industrial nation. Waging war in the U.S. represented the opening of a huge job market for a citizenry suffering with unemployment and facing bread lines, soup kitchens, and widespread poverty. Due to mobilization for war, factories flourished; work was available for everyone who sought a job, and, significantly, previously male occupations opened to women. Intense patriotism flared and citizens rallied to contribute to the "war effort."

Post-World War II, Exploration and Experimentation

Immediately after the war, colleges and universities swelled with returning veterans encouraged to further their educations via the G.I. Bill of Rights. This monetary program benefited the service men and women and benefited financially challenged schools, among them schools of aviation. The late 1940s and the 1950s, most U.S. citizens, although grieving at the loss of so many servicemen and women, recognized the good fortune in having escaped devastation to our homeland. Economic growth saw families moving from urban areas to nearby suburban areas, swelling housing markets and painting a new image of prosperity and material comfort. The American Dream, which once had been the national ideal of the freedom to pursue life, liberty, and happiness, metamorphosed into a more materialistic concept— that of owning a home, property, and an automobile or two.

Yet, as the Fifties began, hard-won peace proved tenuous; it wasn't long before the cloud of Communist imperialism blackened skies. In 1950, Chinese Communists invaded Tibet and North Korean Communists invaded South Korea. In response to a United Nations' request, President Harry S. Truman ordered U.S. military personnel to Korea. Truman also reacted to the Communist threat in Vietnam and signed a military assistance pact with France, Cambodia, Laos, and Vietnam, sending arms to Saigon with military advisors as weapons instructors. U.S. citizens were again embroiled in violent conflicts.

Parallels Converged

To achieve proper perspective in fine art, parallels appear to converge at a vanishing point on the horizon. Similarly, the Fifties and the Sixties resulted in the convergence of two ideologies: the hip culture, which protested inequities and ridiculed conformity to mainstream society, paralleled capitalistic ingenuity, determination, and energy. In technology, U.S. scientists and engineers soared with their quests for speed and transportation efficiency and nurtured an intense competition with Russia for supremacy in aerospace. As drastic changes swirled through the cultural fabric of the United States; its citizens continued to explore, to invent, and to profit. As the diverse parallels converged, they formed a strong dynamic.

The dichotomy was evident in literature. In 1957, Jean-Louis "Jack" Kerouac coined the phrase "Beat Generation" by publishing *On The Road*, an autobiographical and unconventional account of the experiences shared by hitchhikers crossing our nation, primarily inspired by music, drugs, and sex. The same year, author Ayn Rand championed capitalism and objectivism in *Atlas Shrugged*, cautioning the producers of the world—those who created the wealth—to stand up against those who were content to be takers—those who would redistribute the fruits of others' minds and ingenuity. She proclaimed man's noblest activity to be "productive achievement."

The year 1957 also inaugurated the era of the jet plane. The Boeing 707-120 made its debut as the first U.S.-built passenger jet aircraft in commercial transportation. This 600 mile-per-hour aircraft carried passengers greater distances and at dramatically faster speeds in less time. More citizens were encouraged to travel, which led to a need for more commercial pilots.

And 1957 heralded another auspicious first: On 9 September 1957, Congress passed the first U.S. civil rights bill since the days of the post-Civil War reconstruction and established a Civil Rights Commission. Women were among the minorities with grievances over inequality in economic, educational, and social issues; voices for equality were being heard.

"The Sixties"

The 1960s, rather than falling within the expected limits of a decade, became a far-reaching era, spanning more than ten years and spawning winds

of change, of choice, and of opportunity. A time of affluence for the nation, the Sixties writhed in conflict and agitation; it contrasted times of economic health with societal revolt and times of unparalleled scientific achievements with cultural upheaval. On one hand, society churned against the "establishment," against authority, discrimination, and the U.S. involvement in Vietnam. On the

Emily "flies" the United Air Lines CAE simulator, which held an important place in her career.

4

other, technological ingenuity, inventiveness, and progress ascended breathtaking heights. As civil rights demonstrations pushed minorities— including women—into the forefront for justice, engineers and scientists produced more powerful jet aircraft and landed Buzz Aldrin and Neil Armstrong on the earth's moon. What a verdant period for a young woman— Emily Hanrahan Howell Warner—to flourish and grow.

While we were rocked and rolled musically, taunted with the lure of mind-expanding substances, and piqued by adherents of the literature of the anti-conventional Beatniks, there was a parallel percussion. The 1960s pulsed with the work ethic fathered at America's inception. A capitalistic, inventive spirit marched while the counterculture gyrated. Though seemingly pitted against one another, both movements had merits. Perhaps the confrontations of "The Sixties" will best be answered in the future as U.S. citizens and their government officials find ways to unite the best of capitalism and social programs and to discard the worst features of each.

In 1961, the Russians were first with their cosmonaut Yuri Gagarin and the U.S. followed with astronaut Alan Shepard, both countries rocketing their men to outer space. That which had once seemed to be science fiction became a highly competitive and frenzied race for space.

It is an intriguing and little known fact that an outstanding American woman pilot, Betty Skelton, made history as a first. In 1959, two years before Shepard's flight, Skelton became the first U.S. woman to undergo numerous NASA tests in the possibility that women pilots might be selected as astronauts for Project Mercury. This program and the succeeding Project Gemini with a spacecraft built for two astronauts explored human survival in space. Betty Skelton's ultimate dream was to participate in the space program. Featured by LOOK magazine in a cover story in February 1960 and successful in the testing to which she was put, Betty was allowed to go no further in the space program. She admitted, "Unfortunately, in 1959, the last thing on NASA's mind was to select a woman for the program, and the first woman to venture into space (and not as a pilot), was nearly 25 years later."

The USSR put a woman into space on 16 June 1963. Betty Skelton Frankman and the Mercury 13, thirteen women who also passed astronaut testing soon after Betty, waited 20 years for the first U.S. woman to follow suit. Can they draw meager consolation from the fact that their achievements opened doors for those women, like Emily, who followed?

Betty Friedan's book, *The Feminine Mystique*, was published in 1963 and women began to organize, articulating their demands for equality and finding kindred spirits across the nation. In Friedan, a journalist who knew her way around labor protests and who articulated fair labor practices intelligently and persuasively, the women's liberation movement discovered its champion. She was instrumental three years later in forming NOW, the National Organization of Women.

Although Wilbur Wright died prematurely in 1912, Orville Wright lived to 1948, witnessing the fantastic growth of aviation to and during World War II; he lived to be astounded at technology's great leaps. In 1903, he could have had no inkling that, within sixty years, what he referred to as a flying machine would take the shapes of jumbo jets, supersonic transports, and space shuttles. Nor could he envision the social and political wave that broke on the shores of the United States not long after Rosa Parks defied the requirement that she rise and give her seat on a bus to a white passenger in December of 1955. Her arrest fueled a massive boycott and her indomitable spirit became a symbol for organized protests.

Ratification of the Equal Rights Amendment (ERA) in approximately 35 states meant that, in participating states, rights could not be denied on the basis of gender. Mrs. John Adams had, in 1776, requested that male citizens not be given unlimited power. She advocated vigorously that women be allowed to vote, to own property, to keep their own wages, and to have custody of their own children. Abigail Adams would have appreciated the ERA addressing gender rights and that, although 188 years too late, the Civil Rights Act of 1964 prevented employers from discriminating in hiring practices on the basis of gender.

In the 1970s, when then-Secretary of Defense Les Aspin announced that women could be trained as combat pilots and newspapers headlined the training of the U.S. Air Force's "First Women Military Pilots," members of the World War II Women Airforce Service Pilots (WASP) were insulted. They campaigned for recognition as military veterans and, better late than never, thirty years after their terms of service, the 1977 Congress awarded veteran status to members of the WASP. In 1984, each was awarded the Victory Medal and those who served for more than a year received the American Theater Medal. Every WASP heralded the news that military combat piloting was opened to women. They also secured their rightful place as the pioneers who made that decision possible, the pioneers who opened the doors for modern military women pilots.

Emily took to the air, the right woman in the right place and at the right time. Here, as First Officer at the controls of a Convair 580, she was perfectly suited to open the cockpit for herself and for others.

7

Emily Hanrahan Howell Warner is humble and is also proud that, like her mentors, the WASPs, she opened the first door into the world of U. S. commercial aviation so that today's woman airline pilot can take her rightful place in the sky. Like the thirty years that lapsed after WWII and before the WASPs were recognized as having served in their country's military forces, thirty years elapsed after a few women briefly took to the skies in the 1930s before Emily's career became a reality.

What a difference the convergence of social and technological change meant. As women's achievements became recognized and appreciated and advances in aviation lured millions of travelers to the skies, opportunities were created in which talented women could flourish. In Denver, Colorado, Emily, although never resorting to legal battles, definitely benefited. A burgeoning growth in aviation brought a need for more pilots and the push for economic equality for women opened doors that had been barred. Both contributed to the fertile climate in which Emily found career opportunities. Both made it possible for her to be the first woman to be hired as an airline pilot in the scheduled airline fleet, to enter a career in what had been an all-male domain, and to ensure a unique place in history.

During her career, Emily flew this Convair 580, the de Havilland DHC-6 Twin Otter, the Boeing 737, and the Boeing 727. As a flight instructor, there were few General Aviation aircraft that she did NOT fly.

CHAPTER 2: FIRST STEPS, FIRST FLIGHT

Emily's family roots were deep in Irish soil and Emily will often admit that she's "as Irish as Paddy's Pig." On her maternal side, the Boyles trace to Longford, Ireland in the County of Westmeath and to Waterford, home of the famed crystal factory. One of the Boyle ancestors married into the family that traces its lineage to Sir Robert De Poer. Among the invaders of Ireland in 1172 and arriving with King Henry the Second, Sir Robert was granted the city of Waterford by charter. The same King Henry brought to Ireland a Papal document of authority from the only English Pope ever elected—Pope Adrian. Emily's heritage is auspicious.

It has not been established that she could trace her roots to the famed Robert Boyle, the Irish scientist who, in 1662, formulated Boyle's Law and was interested in the density and properties of gas. Yet, Boyle's Law and the findings that bear his name, that the volume of gas is inversely proportional to pressure at a constant temperature, are certainly basic to the air, the realm in which Emily has spent some of her happiest hours.

In 1929, Emily's mother, Emily Violet Boyle, married John William Hanrehan, whose name derived from the Gaelic "O'Hanraghan." The name

has undergone a series of spelling changes that continue in Emily's family to this day. Two of her brothers spell it as their father did, with an "e." Eileen and Emily chose to spell their name with an "a," Hanrahan.

Emily Violet Boyle Hanrehan and John William Hanrehan, Emily's parents.

In ancient Irish history, Hanrehans were lords of a territory in County Westmeath and chiefs in a district in the present county of Tipperary, the site from which Emily's paternal great-great-grandfather, Joseph Hanrehan, emigrated. He and his family are believed to have left Ireland during the time of the disastrous "potato famine of 1845-1850," a scourge that was social and economic in its source and exacerbated by the blight that blackened and withered healthy potato crops. Many fled to escape starvation. Other hundreds were evicted from the land; some were paid to emigrate. More than a million peasants died and another million left to start life anew on other shores. Like the scattering of Scots to make room for more sheep during the dreaded "Clearances" of land in Scotland, many Irish men, women, and children heeded the cry, "Quit Ireland or Perish!"

It is significant that the strength of purpose and determination of those who came before continues to be reflected in their offspring. Emily's ancestors found passage to the United States and, grateful for the challenge and the opportunity to obtain 160 acres of public land under the Homestead Act passed by the U.S. Congress in 1862, they settled in Minnesota. To abide by the rules of the Homestead Act, they claimed the land as their own after having resided on it and cultivated it for five years after an initial claim. Some of the family homesteads remained in the family for more than 135 years.

Wartime Formative Years

Emily's father John, who suffered with asthma, left Minnesota for Denver seeking the drier climate for his health. It was in the midst of the Great Depression and John Hanrehan was fortunate to be among the employed, although his meager wages from his job with Railway Express were thinly spread in caring for his growing family. Three boys, Jack, Patrick, and Dick were born during the decade that preceded the birth of their twin sisters, Emily and Eileen, on 30 October 1939. A younger brother, Dennis, completed the family. Because their mother, a Mezzo Soprano who sang with the Denver Opera Company, sang 6 o'clock mass every morning for thirty years, and their father left early for his work, a great deal of responsibility fell to Jack as the eldest. Jack saw to it that Pat, Dick, Eileen, Emily, and Dennis were readied for school. As soon as he was able to hold a job, he shared his earnings, giving the younger children money to buy ice cream cones at the creamery. When there was a chance for Eileen and Emily to go skiing with classmates, he bought their first pairs of ski pants. Eventually, when Eileen wanted to go to nursing school, Jack saw to it that she had the money to attend.

Patrick, William, Emily, Jack, and Dick flank the youngest, Dennis, Eileen, and Emily, in the family portrait taken in the early 1950s.

Significant parallels existed between aviation advances and Emily's life. Emily's birth year—1939—saw the brilliant Igor Sikorsky, fervent in his quest to create a useful helicopter, design and personally pilot the first practical helicopter – the VS-300. The same year heralded the first North Atlantic

11

airmail service and the first trans-Atlantic passenger service started by Pan American Airways, which also completed the first flight of a fortnightly service of the "California Clipper" between San Francisco and Auckland, New Zealand.

Emily was barely a month old when the United States felt some of the earliest ramifications of what would become a global war—the lifting of an embargo against arms shipments that released $170,000,000 worth of orders for American-built airplanes from France and Great Britain. Despite its isolationism and unilateralism, clouds of war darkened over the U.S. as Germany invaded Poland in 1939 and our allies, England and France, declared war on the Fascists. The Civilian Pilot Training Program (CPTP), which later became the War Training Service (WTS), was initiated at numerous locations across the nation in a quest to create a cadre of pilots for the pending worldwide war. Many U.S. citizens flocked to England to do their part— men set an example by forming the unique Eagle Squadrons, cadres of U.S. pilots flying for Britain's Royal Air Force, and women like Helen Richey volunteered to fly for the British Air Transport Auxiliary (ATA).

After Japanese airplanes bombed not only Pearl Harbor, but several islands in the Pacific Ocean on the same fateful day of 7 December 1941, America responded quickly and resolutely. In U.S. homes, patriotism was the focus and citizens like Emily's family went all-out for "the war effort." Gasoline was rationed, fruit and vegetable gardens, "Victory Gardens," were planted in backyards, ration stamps were treasured and used as sparingly as possible, and citizens volunteered willingly to do more than their share.

Although she was very young, the events of World War II had enormous influence on Emily as they did on all who lived through the times. Cousins, brothers, fathers, uncles, husbands, aunts, mothers, sisters, and wives were inexorably involved. Lives were put on hold. Lives were lost. No family went unscathed.

In the aftermath of war, aviation reflected the enormous growth that resulted from the reaction to hostilities. In 1945, as Emily was starting into primary school, Air Transport Command started the first round-the-world air service and a Douglas C-54 flew 23,147 miles in 149 hours from Washington, DC around the globe to return to Washington. While Emily attended grade school, man flew faster than the speed of sound and the aircraft that would later figure so importantly in her life, the Douglas Aircraft Super DC-3, made its first test flight on 23 June 1949. A month later, the first flight of the de Havilland Comet prototype heralded the beginnings of commercial jet air travel.

Emily's older brothers had been too young to be drafted for military service, but each family member knew the meaning of sacrifice. They did a great deal of walking, used public transportation, found odd jobs, and eked out

a humble living. After 1945, the twins and their younger brother, Dennis, walked to their parochial school, St. Catherine's. The girls rarely dressed alike unless their mother could find matching chicken feed sacks from which to make their dresses. She purposefully searched through sacks of feed

13

for just such matching fabric, expending the feed on the chickens that lived in the backyard and provided eggs for their meals.

Emily said, "I was always conscious of our poverty. Children can be extremely cruel to other children and, because others made us painfully aware that we had less than some, Eileen and I weren't very happy in grammar school. Yet, our mother did her very best to encourage us to be proud and to have some dignity. She always made the most of what we had. She found it possible, for example, to take us to see the operas in which she performed because she was part of the cast. She instilled a lifelong love of good classical music in each of us.

At their graduation from eighth grade at St. Catherine's Elementary School, twins Emily and Eileen posed with their proud mother (on the previous page) and with their priest, Father Lemieux.

"Making a big deal of the fact that her girls were twins, Mother was always on the lookout for promotions that were advantageous. There were two sets of twins skating in the Ice Follies and, when they performed in Denver, a "twin day" meant free tickets for us. Occasionally there were free tickets to movie matinees offered to twins. Mother never failed to take advantage of such opportunities to introduce something extra in our lives."

Their father, who also sought ways to expand his children's horizons, was able to obtain free passes for the railroad and took the children on train trips. Emily remembers traveling to visit their many relatives in Minnesota. As their mother was one of a family of twelve and their paternal grandfather had sired seven children, a joyful confusion of uncles, aunts, and cousins greeted them. Free train trips to Minnesota were events to anticipate eagerly and to enjoy to the fullest.

In Colorado, her mother arranged for her younger children to attend a charity summer camp, Santa Maria, in Bailey, just west of Denver. Emily remembered, "Attendance there required an application and proof that we were a needy family. Somehow, that made me feel even poorer. It was as if we were asking for favors. But, Mother got the job done and the experiences for her children were among the best in our lives."

Attending Camp Santa Maria four years in a row taught Emily an enduring love of the Rocky Mountains. There, she attended chapel every morning, and enjoyed the two weeks of swimming, hiking, riding, camping. She permanently etched into her mind's eye the beauty of clear mountain dawns and crimson sunsets that bathed the mountain peaks in a fiery glow. The first love of her life was the good-looking young wrangler at the camp who was responsible for the care of the horses. He saw to it that she got the best horse to ride and Emily developed a lifelong love of horses and horseback riding.

As Emily started into high school in 1953, test pilot A. Scott Crossfield flew at Mach 2—twice the speed of sound. Emily was not yet following such record-setting events, but the time would come.

During grade school, Emily had been both impressed and embarrassed that her mother could whip muslin feed sacks into school clothes. Attendance at the parochial Holy Family High School meant wearing required school uniforms, the "great equalizers." Uniforms protected Emily and other students from clothes that carried any stigma of poverty. Whereas she had not felt a sense of belonging in grade school, she eased into high school and began to take part in activities. She became a member of the ski club, sang in the church choir, and volunteered charitably with the Little Sisters of the Sick Poor.

"I learned to admire and respect several of my teachers," she said, "Sister Margaret Ann, my chemistry teacher, and Sister Mildred Gerard, who was convinced that I would be a fine nun some day. I'd not been encouraged toward any special career or calling by anyone else. I'd always been religious and caring, so the thought of becoming a nun was not outside the realm of possibility."

Taking Latin and the sciences, Emily especially enjoyed chemistry and was in awe of another favorite, Sister Mary Rhodes, her English teacher. She said, "I appreciated all that Sister Mary Rhodes inspired in me and will always revere her for having introduced me to Antoine de St. Exupéry and his classic, *Wind, Sand and Stars*, written the year that I was born. Assigned as required reading, we discussed how it reflected St. Exupéry's philosophy. It was my first introduction to a sensitive, compelling, literary description of flight and flying. Poetic in its style, the book resonated with me."

Wind, *Sand and Stars* took Emily aloft on his early airmail flights and on to his crash landing on the arid desert in Libya. She was intrigued that St. Exupéry considered the airplane as a means of centering himself in reality. She analyzed the risks that he championed and the bravery that was real as he dealt with the concept of death.

Emily's bedroom on the second floor of their home faced the east. As a teenager, she began to notice long strings of lights in the sky and discovered that they were the landing lights of airplanes that were approaching Denver's Stapleton Airport. She watched them each evening before falling asleep. Then, on Christmas Eve, "a night when it wasn't easy for any young person to fall asleep, I noticed an airplane that flew by with a large Christian Cross illuminated on its side. Later, I discovered that it was a Frontier Airlines DC-3 that was lit for the spirit of Christmas, an annual gift to the people of Denver for years. Still later, I also discovered that the glowing holiday DC-3 was the brainchild of Frontier Captain Everett Aden, with whom I flew. Captain Aden, who referred to me as 'one of the fellas,' became one of my mentors."

Emily's childhood home.

Lacking the $7.50 to buy a uniform to be part of the Holy Family High School Pep Club, a fourteen-year-old Emily walked with some friends past a drug store across the street from the school. She teased, "I'll bet I could get a job in there," and she was dared to try. Mr. Woodman, the proprietor, hired her and Emily started working for him three days a week. "Between dealing with customers and selling perfume and Mr. Woodman's prescriptions, I learned a lot. Best of all, I earned my own money, was able to join the Pep Club, and started to develop the sense of independence that I still cherish. It wasn't long after that I applied to work as a salesgirl at Denver's May Company. I worked at that lovely department store, today transformed into the Adam's Mark Hotel, throughout the rest of high school."

During the summer, she was hired to sell cotton candy at Lakeside Amusement Park. She said, "It was like going to a party every night! As it was a nighttime job, Mother taxied Eileen, who worked at the popcorn concession, and me to and from work. She'd encouraged us to be bus travelers on our own during the days, but nighttime commuting was another story."

One rainy evening that had emptied the amusement park of customers, Emily and her current crush, Russell Riggs, took a ride, stopped for a bite to eat, and returned to the park before it was time for her mother to pick the twins up. Emily said, "Eileen worried the entire time that I was gone. If Mom had caught me, she'd have gotten after Eileen, too. She always held her responsible. Was that fair? No, but that was just the way it was."

Emily, a high school graduate, June 1957

1957—From High School to the Future

Emily graduated from Holy Family with ninety-seven other students in June 1957, the same year that witnessed the first jet flight around the world. Emily and her classmates were being encouraged by their teachers to think in terms of higher education. Emily, especially, was directed toward Loretta Heights College, a Catholic Girls' School, with gentle urging toward becoming a nun. At sessions that she attended at Loretta Heights, she heard discussions about opportunities for girls.

"That was the first I'd ever heard of opportunities for women. I'd not thought previously in terms of a career at all. I'd had aptitude tests that had indicated that I was manually adept and that I'd be a great secretary or bookkeeper, although I never measured up well in the field of nursing. It was a long time before I recognized the slant of the tests toward stereotypic areas traditionally open to women."

Eileen graduated from nurse's training and went on to serve in a distinguished career as a U.S. Air Force nurse. She nursed those wounded in combat during the war in Vietnam.

The twins had been inseparable from birth and, when Eileen decided that she wanted to be a nurse, Emily felt that she had to become a nurse as well. That she became squeamish at the sight of blood and that she hadn't done well in the nursing aptitude tests was of far less importance than her bond with her twin. Fortunately, her job at the May Company sustained her. There she had the chance to see several airline flight attendants, then called stewardesses, shopping during their free time.

"Their lives seemed to exude adventure, travel, and sophistication. I admired them; I even envied them a bit."

When one of her friends asked Emily, "What are you going to do with your life?"

Emily answered impulsively, "I think I'll be a stewardess."

Later she admitted, "The statement just came from nowhere. In addition to those I'd seen at the May Company, one of my cousins was a stewardess for United Air Lines. She had gotten me thinking; but, the minimum age was 21, so I had four years to go. Until I blurted out an answer to my friend, I wasn't even aware that the idea was in my head."

A Dream of Wings

The daughter of a fellow May Company employee attended Western State College, in Gunnison, Colorado. When Emily confided that she might consider becoming a stewardess, the woman suggested, "What would you think of taking an airplane ride? My daughter has mentioned a dance, the Winter Ball, at her college. Why don't you buy a round-trip ticket to Gunnison? I'm sure she can arrange for you to have a date for the ball. You can bunk in the dormitory with her and you'll see a stewardess at work and find out how you like flying in an airplane."

No one in Emily's family had ever flown on a commercial airliner. Interested in free Sunday outings for his family, her father had taken his youngest three—Emily, Eileen, and Dennis—to Rustin Heights, a local Denver airport, fairly often. Emily had loved the sight of the vintage airplanes and she loved seeing the airplanes takeoff and circle to land, almost as if they were in a stylized aerial ballet. To think that she'd have a chance to fly was almost too good to be true. Emily could scarcely believe it. She recognized winds of opportunity and she took advantage of them, a credit to her ingenuity and equally telling of her character.

Pricing Frontier Airline's round-trip air fare between Denver and Gunnison at $28, Emily splurged on a ticket. For an eighteen-year-old high school graduate with no hopes of attending college herself, this planned weekend was an unimaginable thrill. The chance to attend a ball, to date a college man, and to stay in a dormitory were exciting. To be the first in the family to climb aboard a passenger aircraft for flight was the most magical of all.

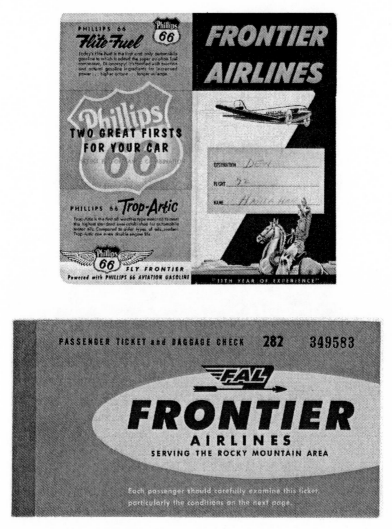

Emily's Frontier Airlines' ticket from Denver to Gunnison, Colorado – more than an adventure, this proved to be the ticket to a lifelong career.

The DC-3 was scheduled to depart at 11:15 on the morning of 30 January 1958 and Emily was more than ready. Her entourage—her father, mother, sister, and brother, Dennis—trooped to the airport, as excited as she. On the way to the airport, her mother mentioned a flight that she had taken with a barnstorming pilot as a young woman in Minnesota. She added, "My father, on the other hand, was cautious. He took out trip insurance from a machine in the airport."

The actual DC-3 in which Emily took her first flight. She'd contemplated becoming a flight attendant, not knowing that a girl could take flying lessons.

The Rockies, an Eagle's Eye View

Emily was alert to every sound, every odor. Surrounded with the airport activities—bags being stowed, a pilot doing a walk-around check of the airplane, refuelers filling the tanks, a stewardess greeting each person who boarded—she felt as if her senses had gone into overdrive. At last, the flight number announced, her family hugged her and wished her well. She waved to them and climbed the boarding stairs. Welcomed by the stewardess and once settled in her seat, she listened to the rhythm of the engines as they coughed into activity and then settled into a synchronized harmony.

As the craft shuddered forward in its taxi, she felt the rocking motion that was not unlike the comfortable gait of a loping horse. Her excitement built as the aircraft turned to take the runway and she felt herself pulled back into her seat. She felt more than heard the increased whine of the engines, the throbbing power; the horse stretched into a full gallop.

The mountains loomed, still off to the left as the airplane headed north. Then the pilot started a gradual right turn to the south, gaining altitude, and positioning his craft on course toward Pueblo. Mountain air, rarely completely smooth, churned and dipped as it sought its way to the plains, rolling away from the Rockies toward the flat lands. This January day the airplane bounced, dipping first the right wing and then the left, rocking into position, climbing for altitude, and affording a panoramic view that stretched from the Flatirons above Boulder toward Pikes Peak near Colorado Springs. Denver's buildings cut jagged sections from the horizon behind them, silhouetted against the earth and the sky.

Emily divided her attention between the stewardess, wondering what it might mean to follow a career such as hers, and taking in the breathtaking views of her Rocky Mountains, mountains that had represented a haven of stability from her earliest recollections. Clouds spilled over the east slope of the Rockies like dollops of whipped cream oozing over strawberry shortcake. Seated on the right side of the airplane, her beloved mountains reached skyward. Whitened with snow that clung to evergreen branches, cupping clouds in the crevasses above the timber line, and defiantly exposing sheer craggy cliffs upon which the snow had no chance to collect, the Rockies symbolized nature's beauty to Emily.

The venerable Douglas design, the DC-3, was born a scant few years before Emily. By the year of her birth, DC-3s carried 75% of all U.S. passengers who took to the air for transportation. Now, nineteen years later, Emily reveled that she was one of those lucky people.

After a stop at Pueblo, the airplane spiraled for sufficient altitude to cross the mountains and to allow for unexpected and invisible turbulence or downdrafts. Once leveled off, the pilot headed toward Gunnison, following canyons carved by the irrepressible rivers flowing from the high country toward the sea.

23

Gunnison, nestled in a beautiful valley, lies south of the Ruby Range of the Elk Mountains and is bordered on the east by the rugged and high Sawatch Range. The canyons and high plateaus south of Gunnison form the eastern portion of the Colorado Plateau. Dams on the Gunnison and the Taylor rivers have created the largest lake in Colorado, the Blue Mesa Reservoir. What would surely be crystal clear blue water during the summer months was now a silvery, icy white. The entire landscape was dusted with white as if by a baker sprinkling powdered sugar on a cake; only isolated evergreen branches broke the monochromatic scheme.

Dorothy's daughter showed Emily a great weekend, introduced her to a good-looking date, and made room for her in the dorm. Yet, the return flight to Denver was Emily's highest priority. On 3 February 1958, Emily proved to be the sole passenger for the 7:30 a.m. departure. In the pale dawn, the snow reflected the shadowy blue of the skies. Emily was enchanted.

A Frontier Airlines DC-3 like that in which a teen-aged Emily took her first flight crosses the snow-capped peaks of the majestic Rocky Mountains. *Photo: Ted Searle.*

"Once we were airborne," she said, "I asked the stewardess if there was any chance that I could go see the cockpit. She checked and, since there were no other passengers, the pilots invited me forward. I absorbed as much as I could, marveling at the gauges, the controls, the switches, and the levers. The pilots had the best jobs of all. Seated for the descent, I felt as if the plane was sliding down a vast invisible staircase. Then, just before touching the ground, it nosed gently up toward the sky. I thought that the plane didn't want the flight to end any more than I did."

In the world of aviation, 1958 was filled with events that later became some of Emily's utmost concerns. Because of the Cold War, funding was more easily obtained for the advancement of aviation and aerospace. There was a tremendous exchange of technological development between the military and the civilian sectors. The winds of change brought what had been inventive forward steps in military aviation and transferred it to the civilian side. Swept-back wings, improved jet engines, increased speed capabilities, and strengthened modern materials enabled great strides in design and were applied to commercial airliners. An air traffic accident over the Grand Canyon two years before – 1956 – had been the catalyst for Congress to pass the Federal Aviation Act of 1958. This legislation created the Federal Aviation Agency that was later changed to the current Federal Aviation Administration (FAA), the agency that would, much later, be Emily's employer. Charged with establishing an air traffic control system, the new agency was also expected to oversee certification of aircraft, airline training, and airline maintenance programs. Airline routes and rates remained under the jurisdiction of the Civil Aeronautics Board. It was also in 1958 that the National Aeronautic and Space Administration (NASA) was born and, the day after Emily's flight, Explorer I, the first U.S. satellite was launched.

Serendipity

Forewarned that her parents wouldn't be able to meet her plane, Emily knew that she had to find the nearest bus stop. After retrieving her small suitcase, she walked in front of the terminal, and hesitated at the curb. A car pulled to a stop beside her and she was surprised to see that the driver was one of the pilots who'd just flown her from Gunnison.

When he offered her a ride, she asked to be dropped off at the bus stop on Colfax Avenue. Emily, still imbued with joy, chattered happily about the flight.

"Well," he said, "if you've discovered that you like flying that much, why don't you take flying lessons?"

Emily gasped. "Can a girl take flying lessons?"

"Sure you can. Go to Clinton Aviation right here at Stapleton Airport. They have a flight school where you can ask some questions and find out all about it. Take a few flying lessons and see how you feel about it once you've had your hands on the controls."

His nudge was just the push that Emily needed and she has always regretted that she never discovered his name. She never adequately thanked him.

Sharing a love of the sky

Ruth Nichols, a well-known pioneering woman pilot, was introduced to Emily at a book-signing for Nichols' biography. The two women shared many qualities, not the least of which is a consuming passion for flying. Nichols, a 1924 graduate of Wellesley who followed graduation with a year off to make her debut into society, had obvious financial advantages to pursue any goals that she chose. Yet, both women had to work hard to accomplish their goals. Both had to forge their own pioneering strides in what had been man's domain. It was fortuitous that Emily had the chance to meet her.

In her book, Nichols asked, "Did I have the right to live my own life? Probably every idealistic girl asks herself this question without finding an easy answer." She went on to say that her mother "despaired of a daughter who preferred the company of 'riffraff' mechanics and barnstormers rather than follow socially accepted rounds. ..." and she exulted, "I loved it all—the smell of the gas and engine oil, the gloom of the cavernous hangars, the shop talk of pilots and mechanics, the spirit of good fellowship and easy camaraderie that prevailed among the members of that exclusive society of airmen."

Emily could have written those words. As she responded to the whispering winds and followed her head and her heart, she, too, "loved it all."

Taken in 1973, Emily and Eileen, two highly successful women.

CHAPTER 3: FLYING LESSONS, THE SKY'S NO LIMIT

Emily was welcomed as a full-time saleswoman at the May Company as soon as she pocketed her high school diploma in June 1957. Surrounded daily by beautifully tailored garments, a wide variety of colorful accessories, jewelry, shoes, the complement of attractive shoppers who frequented her department, and her mother's fine example, Emily was inspired toward self-improvement. She signed up to take several free courses that were offered by the YMCA and some business courses offered by the Emily Griffith Opportunity School. Each widened her perspectives and added more of the qualities that have enhanced her life.

She took a ten-day course in speech and modeling from a woman named Arlene Lamshire and said, "She was fascinating; she gave me lessons in decorum, courtesy, and good manners in addition to proper dress, the right selections of jewelry and scarves, how much to wear and what not to wear depending upon the event—a social night out or a job interview. Ms. Lamshire gave me more than the lessons prescribed—she gave me good start toward self-confidence."

Emily was on a direct line toward becoming a buyer at the May Company. Respected by her superiors, she was being groomed for promotion. Then, in February 1958, just a few days after having taken the flight to Gunnison, she took a completely new direction for her life.

1958 – A Pivotal Year

While space probes drew the eyes of the nation's citizens skyward, Emily was one of those who eagerly embraced the idea of flight and flying. An eighteen-year-old with unbridled enthusiasm, Emily followed up on the suggestions of the DC-3 pilot and headed for Clinton Aviation on Denver's

Stapleton Airport. As Shakespeare's Prospero took destiny into his own hands by churning the winds into "The Tempest," Emily was weaving the winds of chance, the winds of change, and the winds of opportunity to create her own career path.

At 18, Emily worked at Denver's May Company to cover one flight lesson a week. She took to the air in "taildraggers" like this Cessna 140.

Flying Lessons

Emily said, "For my first visit to Clinton, I dressed carefully, wanting to make a good impression. I wore a black knit wool dress, a small white French beret, a black wool coat, and a pair of high heels." Although women were not strangers to the Fixed Base Operator (FBO) in Denver, Emily contrasted starkly to the general run of flight school applicants who were casually clad in tennis shoes, jeans, and comfortable sweatshirts. Much later, Clinton Aviation's Chief Pilot, James E. Muncey, who noticed the attractive young woman through the flight school window, said, "I couldn't believe it when I saw you coming across the ramp, dressed to the nines. You looked like someone who just stepped out of a fashion magazine."

To her, "A Frontier pilot told me that I might take flying lessons here," Jim Muncey patiently responded. He told her about flying lessons, what they entailed, the cost per flying hour, the requirements for acquiring her Private Pilot certificate, and asked her how often she could fly. He explained what every prospective flight student heard, "You will start off with an instructor and, after several dual flights, and the instructor will gradually turn more and more of the responsibility for safe flight to you, based on judgment of your progress."

He told her about the airplanes that were based at Clinton and about the aviation ground school that would coincide with the actual flying, "...to prepare you to take the written test that has to be passed before you can take a practical flight test."

Not once in the conversation was there even a hint that women weren't welcome as student pilots at Clinton Aviation. In fact, Muncey told Emily about another woman pilot, a flight instructor.

Emily asked about the possibility of flying every Tuesday, her regular day off from her job at the May Company. Telling her that he would personally instruct her in a Cessna 140, November 101 Whiskey, he scheduled her for the following week.

At $12.75 per flight hour for the airplane rental, Emily made some rapid calculations. With her monthly salary of $152 from the May Company and the $20 per month paid to her parents for room and board, she tried to assess whether the $81 remaining, after she'd paid monthly flying costs of $51, would cover her additional expenses.

With her characteristic directness, Emily broke the news of having checked into flying lessons to her parents that night at dinner. She recalled, "They were skeptical; although, at that time, they were skeptical when I wanted to buy a new dress! Whenever I'd come home with something new – shoes, a hat, a pocketbook, a scarf – my mother would ask, 'How much did that cost?'

"I learned to tell white lies. Invariably, I'd lower the price because I knew that, whatever the price, the next comment would be, 'That's a foolish way to spend money.'"

All who suffered through the full impact of the Great Depression were left with permanent recollections of economic collapse, bank closures, and the loss of one's savings and Emily's parents were extremely practical and frugal. Although, as Emily was the last of their children to leave home and start supporting themselves, they were certainly more comfortable financially than they had been with six mouths to feed.

But, flying lessons? Unable to imagine aviation as a career path for their daughter, they saw no future in flying lessons. To complicate matters, Emily's twin sister's choice of a nursing career relegated the comparative flying lessons to the realm of the frivolous.

Emily was resolute, insisting, "I'd just like to try a few lessons." Her mother ultimately and reluctantly agreed. Her father simply said, "Be careful."

Would Emily have gone against her mother's wishes had she adamantly forbidden flying lessons? She said, "Luckily, I never had to make that decision. My older brothers had all gone off to their own pursuits. Eileen was training as a nurse. I was only eighteen and still living at home; but, Mother had watched three of her sons and Eileen leave her nest. She knew that it was only a matter of time before I would be ready to leave home, too. I was lucky to have had older brothers and a twin. Mother wasn't overawed with any scheming on my part."

Had they taken a hard stand and steadfastly refused to give her a chance, Emily probably would have gone against their wishes. She was bursting with curiosity. She recalled wanting to pursue modeling courses after she'd completed Ms. Lamshire's, "I enjoyed her ten-day modeling course so much that I wanted to pursue modeling and I made some inquiries at the Morganti School of Charm and Modeling. Told that courses in speech, ballet exercise, and modeling would total $300, I spoke with my mother. I extolled the virtues of learning to be poised and graceful and the benefits of earning money as a model and told her that I'd really like to take the course.

"She dismissed it, again saying it was a foolish waste of money. But, comforting myself that she never forbid me, I enrolled in the classes anyway. I told the owner, Cesare Morganti, that I couldn't pay in one lump sum, so he allowed me to make payments out of my salary. To the time of her death, my mother and I never spoke of it. I don't think she ever knew that I went ahead and pursued the lessons.

"I've never regretted nor have I felt guilty about defying my mother's wishes. Her love was music. She taught singing to young women and I'm sure that every one of them was better for having taken her lessons. I gained poise from modeling; I even earned a bit of money as a model. Modeling didn't become my career choice, but it enhanced the career path that I followed."

Emily amassed more than 4,000 flying hours in the Cessna 150/152.

Taking to the Skies

Emily embarked on her adventure on 6 February 1958. Never in her wildest imagination did she consider that to the day fifteen years later, on 6 February 1973, she would make her first flight as an airline pilot with Frontier Airlines.

A light snow was falling and low clouds clung to the mountains as she took the bus to Stapleton Airport on 6 February. Muncey, having seen the disappointment on her face at the thought of canceling the lesson due to the weather, suggested that they taxi around on the ramp for a while. He went to great pains to give her a good grounding in the handling of an aircraft and the flight control surfaces. When he discovered that she didn't drive a car, he was actually pleased. "That's good," he said. "You won't have any bad habits that have to be unlearned. It is easier to learn to operate the controls correctly at the start rather than having to undo ingrained habits. It is important that you correctly use your feet on the rudders."

He walked around the craft with her, performing the necessary preflight check, and then talked with her briefly while they sat inside the small cabin. He showed her the ailerons, the elevators, and the rudder, explaining how they were to be used. After the engine fired into life and the cockpit filled with the rhythmic sound of power, he demonstrated taxi and gave her the chance to follow suit. A fatherly and experienced instructor, Muncey exuded patience, even when she hammered the brakes and momentarily lost directional control of the Cessna on the hard-packed snow. The aircraft started to slew.

"I've got it," he said, quickly easing off the power, moving the yoke back and making firm contact between the tailwheel and the ground. Emily received one of her first introductions to the basics of control.

By 18 February, Emily's Student Pilot Certificate (attesting to a medical exam by a physician licensed to give flight physicals) was tucked into her wallet. Each Tuesday she showed up for her flight hour and slowly accrued time and experience. "I was having a ball," she said. "In fact, I was having so much fun, Munce told me that I'd have to settle down and start taking it all more seriously. I could scarcely wait for each succeeding week and the flying lesson that promised to be its highlight."

By August of 1958, having learned to drive and obtaining her driving license, she bought a Deluxe Pontiac for $300. "I'd been taking the bus and felt that it would be much easier to travel between the May Company, home, and the airport if I were to own my own car. Besides, I'd augmented my salary with some modeling, hostessing for a few political campaigns like that of Mark Hogan in Denver."

One year later, in the summer of 1959, a secretarial-receptionist position opened at Clinton Aviation. Emily jumped at the chance. Her superior at the

May Company, Juanita Beatty, warned, "You are making a mistake to leave us now. You have a future here. I hate to see you do this.'"

Nonetheless, Emily gave a two-week notice and started earning $350 per month at Stapleton Airport. By 1961, her salary increased to $550 per month. Within six years she earned $650 and, when she started making application to fly with the airlines, her salary had reached $850. Much later, she received a note from Juanita Beatty who wrote, "You certainly knew what you were doing!"

Emily is flanked by her flight instructor, Jim Muncey, on the left and a fellow instructor, Jay Barnwell. The trio teamed up to lead Clinton Aviation.

Flying in the Colorado Rockies can be a challenge to lowland pilots, accustomed to the performance of small two- or four-place training airplanes operating from low elevations in relatively predictable wind patterns. The winds churning over, around, and among the peaks of the mountains can be compared to river rapids swirling and billowing against rocks and tree-laden banks. The pilot who learns to fly from an elevation of 5,000 feet above sea level – and Denver is the "Mile High City" – learns not only to deal with the capricious winds of the mountains, but also the rarer air density of higher elevations. It was as fortuitous for Emily to become skillful in mountainous terrain as a student as it was for her to learn to taxi before driving a car.

In addition to good training, learning came with experience and in profiting from mistakes. Emily lost control of her Cessna 140 during her third solo flight.

"I'd encouraged my mother to come out to Sky Ranch, a small airport in east Denver, for her first chance to see me fly. I told her that I'd planned to make three landings at Sky Ranch, and then I'd return to Stapleton Airport where she could pick me up.

"My three landings at Sky Ranch were fine. However, when I returned to Stapleton, the wind was blowing at 12 knots out of the Southwest and, although I'd been taught to hold the elevator all the way back to keep the tailwheel firmly on the ground, I relaxed my control. The tail rose in a gust of wind that spun us around during the landing, dipping a wing.

"Luckily, my mother was still en route; she missed seeing my groundloop. But, there I was blocking the runway at Stapleton. I was really worried. I thought my flying career was over before it had hardly begun."

Clinton Aviation mechanics brought the aircraft into the shop while Emily sat in the office, her heart the heaviest it had been. She met with the FAA's Jim Prendergast and with her instructor, Jim Muncey. Although she dreaded the answer, she asked, "Will I ever be allowed to fly again?'"

The men explained to Emily that a groundloop often results in damage to a wingtip or, if extreme, to the collapse of a gear because of the side-loads imposed upon it. They also explained that it generally happens to those whose experience level is relatively low or to a pilot who fails to continue using proper control inputs from the start to the complete end of a flight. Muncey assured her that she was fortunate, that she'd done minimal damage, and that they'd work it out.

When her mother later asked about the rest of her flight, Emily said, "I told her, 'Just fine.' There was no reason to upset her. I worried that, had she known, she would have made me quit flying."

Accruing time flying cross country, Emily loved the rugged mountains, seeing the Colorado River wending its way through evergreens, and the whitened trunks of aspen. She was blessed with her chances to have an aerial perch. She felt as free as the birds with which she shared the air space and laughed at the clouds with which she danced.

Working in Clinton's front office gave Emily the chance to take free flying opportunities when they came along. On 17 December 1960, the 57th anniversary of the first powered flight by the Wright Brothers, Emily grabbed the chance to fly Operation Air Watch. Air Watch proved to be "free flying," as her job was to fly above the highways of Denver with reporters announcing traffic conditions over the radio.

Flight instructors train pilots from the right seat, using dual controls and seating the student pilot in the left seat, or pilot-in-command position. Emily amassed more than 7,000 flying hours as an instructor prior to being hired by Frontier.

With this can-do attitude, Emily logged 337 flight hours in completing her airman's diary, her first logbook. Between 1958 and 1962, she earned two certificates and two ratings: passing the written tests, flight tests, and accumulating the necessary flight experience to advance from Private Pilot (on

6 March 1959), to a Commercial Pilot Certificate (on 12 February 1960), and to add the rating of Certificated Flight Instructor-Airplane (on 18 September 1961). When Emily moved from the left seat to the instructor's position of right seat, she had amassed 220 hours of total time, 137 hours of solo flight time, and countless hours of joy.

Tempering Joy

Some pleasure was tarnished when the country's first Irish-Catholic president, John F. Kennedy, was assassinated in Dallas, Texas in 1963. Emily, who identified closely with her own Irish-Catholic roots, joined millions of citizens in mourning.

Some of her joy of flight was a bit tarnished, too, when, soon after becoming a Private Pilot, she flew her younger brother Dennis as her first passenger. "We flew to Rustin Heights Airport where our father had taken us for outings when we were children. I landed, finding too late that the strip was muddier than it had looked from the air. When I turned around to taxi back to the end of the short runway, the hair rose on the back of my neck. I'd learned about short field takeoffs and knew that the mud could cause drag during takeoff and, as we started the takeoff roll, my worry became acute. The aircraft was terribly sluggish, acting almost as if it couldn't pull itself out of the muck to take off at all.

"When we reached the barest necessary flight speed, I hauled it off the ground, pushing the nose forward to gain airspeed. There were power lines straight ahead at the end of the runway. We barely squeaked over them. Later, I admitted to Dennis that I'd done one of the dumbest things I'd ever done. We were really lucky to have made it over those lines. He and I agreed that Someone was flying with us that day."

Having accepted another chance for a free flight, Emily soloed a Clinton Aircraft to another field to display it at an air show. Another valuable lesson came her way during the return flight. An enormous cumulonimbus cloud blackened her path of flight with a dark, angry mass of cloud, wind, and rain. "Trying to skirt the storm, I cut the wrong way. The storm raced its way eastbound and I went eastbound. I should have given it time to pass and flown to the west behind it. However, the storm kept closing in on me, keeping the pressure on for me to continue flying farther and farther to the east.

"It gives you a sinking feeling to have the throttle to the firewall and to see that a storm can move as fast as or faster than you can. I was about 45 minutes late getting back to Stapleton; but, in the long run, I was lucky that it didn't overtake me. That thunderstorm taught me an important lesson."

Every bit of experience counted toward Emily's future – on the job and in her private life. After having become a flight instructor in 1961, Emily accrued flight hours and, as is typical of most teachers, she found that the teaching itself enhanced her own skills. She not only instructed at Clinton, she was called upon to instruct at a short, dirt airstrip in the mountains. For her freelance flight instructing, she was given the chance to fly a Bonanza that belonged to one of her students.

She often flew back and forth between Denver and the mountain airstrip because it was located near the cabin that she and her siblings had pitched in to buy as a family retreat. The rustic cabin was nestled into the hills near Winter Park, the popular ski resort, and near Grand Lake, the headwaters of the Colorado River. The area gave Emily immense pleasure, but also was almost the scene of her death.

In the retractable geared Bonanza, she took off one hot afternoon to give a sightseeing ride to a man, his wife, and their child. "I learned about Aircraft Performance and Density Altitude in one close scrape. The temperatures were in the mid-eighties and the airstrip was at an elevation of 8,600 feet. I took off to the west into the wind, but should have reversed that takeoff direction as the elevations actually break away and are lower to the east. Here we were. There were power lines at the end of the runway, just as there had been in my flight with Dennis. Instinct told me that I was in trouble the instant we got airborne. There was no air. It was like a tea kettle that has solid water inside of the kettle, but as soon as it turns to steam, whoosh, there is nothing there! The power lines were growing blacker and larger by the second.

"Somehow I knew that I couldn't change a single thing. If I were to raise the gear, I'd have the moment of sink prior to the airplane taking advantage of the reduced drag. I held steady, sweating profusely. We just made it over the wires, but my troubles weren't over. I couldn't coax the Bonanza to climb. I headed for the forest, figuring it would be cooler over the trees and we staggered for a while until the airplane finally began to catch up. To myself, I chanted, 'You dumb shit! You dumb shit!' but I never said anything to the people in the airplane. There was no reason for everyone to be nervous about the outcome of the flight!"

In the same Bonanza another time, Emily was picking the aircraft up for its owner in San Francisco (SFO), skirting the Rockies to the south to deliver the aircraft to Denver. Climbing out of SFO, she clawed for altitude to get above heavy clouds. The flight was fairly uneventful "on top" at approximately 17,000 feet to the skies above New Mexico before the weather continued to deteriorate and she became surrounded by clouds: "socked in."

She said, "Up to that flight, I hadn't worked with Distance Measuring Equipment (DME) very often. I grabbed a chart and, with it spread across my lap, I drew some lines on it. Then I used the DME and determined that I was close to Shiprock, New Mexico. I knew that the monolith, Shiprock, was the only mountain around there, so I grabbed the chance to descend through a hole in the clouds, hoping that it wasn't a 'sucker hole.' I felt fairly secure on the descent and was relieved to break through below the clouds near Farmington. I landed and, as the stormy weather continued, I bought a ticket on a Frontier flight and left the Bonanza sheltered in Farmington. Aboard the airliner, I asked the altitude of the top of the clouds and discovered that it was 24,000 feet. That was above the service ceiling of the Beech. I never could have climbed that high. I was lucky to find the hole and get down in Farmington in one piece."

When Emily flew Air Watch, she was supposedly sharing the free flying with all of the other Clinton instructors. Many of the male instructors, however, didn't care for the repetitious flying. When they offered the flights to Emily, she never refused. She discovered that flying is never dull. One time the weather closed in from the west, almost obscuring the airport in blowing snow. In another incident, she recalled landing behind a TransWorld Airlines Super Connie. "That was the worst turbulence that I'd ever encountered. It might have been the three rudders behind that plane or maybe I just got too close. It was really rough and I took the airplane around. Flights like that had a way of scaring the radio reporters who flew with me.

"One reporter, Don Martin, had a private license and enjoyed the flying as much as the reporting. One Saint Patrick's Day, I had dyed my hair green as I customarily did each year. Don told the radio audience, 'And this morning, ladies and gentlemen, we have a potted plant aboard.' Then he went ahead to describe my hairdo… a very pretty bright green. Another St. Patrick's Day, similarly greened, I was taken for a ride in a new Cessna helicopter. The pilot touched down, throttling back to let me climb out while the engine was running and get clear of the aircraft before he took off once again. I started out under the spinning blade and all I heard was, 'duck!' I ducked fast because the slowing blade started to dip toward my green head. That was one of my closer calls."

As her flight time accrued, Emily became expert in the airspace of Denver and its surrounds. Even beyond the fact that she was native to Denver, flying gave her a unique way to embrace the city and the mountains as her own.

Thrill Place

Knowing the capriciousness of mountain convective currents and their accompanying turbulence, Emily made it a practice in the summer months to start with her flight students at 4:30 in the morning. The light was dawning, bathing the mountains in a surreal glow, the winds were quiet, and flight students could gain much more than when wrestling for control over updrafts and downdrafts, cross winds, and turbulent roll. She said, "I loved flying in the quiet early hours in the mountains; flying until the temperatures rose and with them the winds, the turbulence, and the high density altitudes. We'd go back again in the evening when calm once again prevailed."

Emily, who was sharing an apartment with her good friend Cecelia Welsh, bought a Pekinese, to her landlord's chagrin. The landlord suggested, gently, since the dog wasn't welcome in the apartment, they had best find another place to live.

"In those days, it was unheard-of for single women to buy houses," explained Emily. "But, I thought, 'Why not?' I found a woman realtor who was willing to take a chance on me and she found a small house for me at 5350 Thrill Place. I was fortunate that my mother had set aside some savings. She loaned me $1,500 and my roommate loaned me $500. I made the down payment, later repaying both of them with interest. Thrill Place lived up to its name; we had lots of fun there.

"My sister, Eileen, who was attending Mercy Hospital School of Nursing, moved in with me, as did some of Eileen's classmates. Thrill Place started to be known as 'Hanrahan's Wild Time Avenue.' We held parties there every weekend. I especially remember a big bash on my twenty-first birthday. Fellows who instructed at Clinton came by as would a group of pilots who flew up from Texas for weekend maneuvers out of Lowry Air Force Base. Lots of times we'd party until two or three in the morning; then, I'd jump in the bathtub, clean up, and go to the airport to start the day's flying. We had amazing energy levels. I'd work until noon, go home and crash, then get up and repeat the performance. Those days were fun."

Stanley Howell

Accustomed to seeing many more men than women show an interest in flight training, it came as a bit of a surprise to Emily that one particular man made an impression on her. She gave Stan Howell the customary introductory flight in 1962 and introduced him to the flight instructor who would be in charge of his program. Stan's good looks attracted Emily, but even more attractive was his pleasant disposition. "Stan did everything right. He couldn't have been more polite. He waited an appropriate time before asking me out, and then took me to dinner at Trader Vic's. We had a delightful first date. A member of the Colorado National Guard, Stan was a nurse and I identified with the concern that he showed to the people under his care. We enjoyed each other's company and pretty soon we were dating regularly."

After having met Emily's parents, Stan introduced Emily to his mother and his brother, with whom he worked at the nursing home owned by his mother. Emily felt sympathetic when she learned that he and his three brothers had lost their father and that his mother, also a nurse, had been badly hurt in an automobile accident. Hospitalized for quite some time, her three sons grew through their formative years without either parent. Emily said, "Stan was four years older than I and seemed to have his whole act together. When he asked me to marry him, I said yes."

The two were married on 1 June 1963; but, it wasn't long before it became apparent that it wasn't a simple matter to unite two different personalities. Stan worked at night, Emily worked primarily during each day; but also had the responsibility of seeing flight students through their required hours of cross country flight, night flight, and flight test preparation. Both gave of themselves to their work, he to his patients and she to her students. Her schedule was unpredictable and, though they flew together occasionally and Emily helped at the nursing home occasionally, their paths and their temperaments were more divergent than the marriage could stand.

Two years after they were married, Emily was pregnant with their only child. For some couples, this might have brought them closer together; however, for Stan and Emily, that didn't prove to be. Every married couple knows that many things can come between them. Things weren't right; Stan's relationship with his own mother was strained. Perhaps that contributed to relating to a home, a wife, and, now, the concept of family life. The strains took their toll.

Wanting to continue to fly and feeling that she had to keep working, Emily

talked with Jim Muncey, who told her, "Pregnant or no, you can keep on working as long as you feel up to it. You'll be perfectly safe," and he added with a smile, "as long as you can get the elevator back."

Her flying was "perfectly safe," but her marriage, which began with high expectations, began to grow colder than either Emily or Stan wished.

Emily and her son, Stanley Howell, in 1965

A Son is Born

Emily took a six-month leave of absence during which, in April 1965, their son Stanley was born. Emily spent all the time that she could with the baby, knowing that she would be going back to flight training in the near future. She remained at home until June 1965, but she and Stan found that their marriage was untenable. Although they sought help from counselors and Catholic priests, their marriage wasn't to be. Separated when the baby was six months old, they obtained a divorce. It was difficult for all of them, and, Emily, trying to balance motherhood and to earn a full time salary, searched to find good child care for her baby Stanley. She even introduced "Little Stan" to flying when she took him for his first ride on 29 August 1965.

Emily moved to live closer to her mother, who provided loving child care for her grandson, and Emily returned to work on a full time basis. She said, "Munce always held a job open for me whenever I wanted to come back to work. It was more than just lucky; we worked well together to see Clinton Aviation flourish. He was the check pilot who tested my students for their

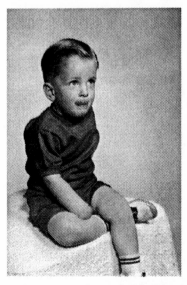

various certificates and he was a good friend upon whom I depended. More than anyone, I have Jim Muncey to thank for encouraging me to be the pilot that I am. As I now was a single mother with a child, my salary became even more essential. Fortunately, a lucrative program lay just around the corner."

A handsome little Stanley turned three.

Denver's Stapleton Airport was home to three scheduled U.S. airlines—Frontier Airlines, Continental Air Lines, and United Air Lines. In 1966, United Air

Lines (UAL) created a test program in which they hired prospective pilots with commercial certificates and a minimum of 160 flying hours. They were required to hold a college degree, but they did not have to be rated in instrument flying. When UAL contracted the trial program with Clinton Aviation, Muncey assigned Emily and two other of his flight instructors to the program.

Stanley's school picture, age five.

In addition to her regular complement of students, Emily was assigned two male students every three weeks. "My job was to get them through instrument training in the three weeks allotted to their training. That was a challenge! We worked two hour blocks. A lot of the guys had come from training that was less than perfect. One of them tried to run me off the runway when we'd just gotten started. He was barely equipped to fly VFR (according to visual flight rules), let alone IFR (according to instrument flight rules). I had to work on his basic skills before we could get the instrument training off the ground."

For two years, Emily flew with this UAL pilot program. She accumulated 1,200 hours a year, 100 hours a month, and, at ten dollars an hour, what she felt was a great salary. She said, "Anytime I flew more than 50 hours a month, I considered it gravy!"

Knowing that all of these men were already destined for airline piloting careers, Emily constantly urged them toward professionalism and excellence. In spite of the incredible gap between their minimal 160 flying hours and her more than 2,000, she respected that they'd been selected for the lucrative career of commercial piloting. With a child to support and awareness of airline pilot salaries, she longed for the same for herself.

Emily was highly respected as a flight instructor and the Chief Pilot of Clinton Aviation. She taught hundreds of men to fly and to aim toward becoming airline pilots.

"I doubt that any airline will ever hire a woman."

In 1967, Emily obtained an interview with Johnny Meyer, then the Chief Pilot with Frontier Airlines. "I explained to Johnny my hopes of becoming an airline pilot and he swung his arm toward a large pile of papers in his in-basket and asked, 'See that stack of applications? There you see 300 applicants wanting to be airline pilots.'

"When he asked about my accumulated flight time and I told him that I had flown approximately 3,000 hours, he made a suggestion. 'I'll tell you what I'd do if I were you,' he said. 'I'd get more multi-engine time and I'd get my Airline Transport Pilot rating.'

"'I'll work on that,' I told him, standing up to leave.

"'But,' he added, 'I doubt that any airline will ever hire a woman.'"

But words never discouraged Emily. She knew enough to turn rejection into acceptance, to answer criticism with excellence. She continued to apply to Frontier, Continental, and United Air Lines—all based in her hometown of Denver. She wouldn't accept that the airlines would never hire a woman.

CHAPTER 4: STARRING IN A MOVIE

Is there any way to measure one person's influence? Can we count the ripples that emanate from the pebble that disturbs a quiet pool? In the 1960s, Emily was introduced to countless aspiring pilots by starring in an instructional movie made by the FAA. Viewers might not have caught her name; they might not even have recognized that she had changed their behavior. But, those interested in flying over the rugged peaks and valleys of U.S. mountain ranges and fortunate enough to see Emily's movie did have modified behavior. They took from the movie that which was important to recall and put it to good use as they ventured out over the Sawtooth, the Cascades, the Uintas, the Sierra Nevada, the Appalachians, the Smokies, or over Emily's beloved Rocky Mountains.

Appropriately entitled "Mountain Flying," the twenty-three minute documentary was filmed at Clinton Aviation. Emily starred as the instructor that she was, projecting a truthful image of a competent and experienced pilot. The FAA wanted her educational film to reach airmen and women, especially those based at low altitude airports, who were unaware of dangers inherent in flying in and around mountainous areas.

Taking her viewers into her cockpit, she described one phenomenon, the foehn winds that can approach at roughly 30 knots (nautical miles per hour) on the windward side of the mountains, only to reach nearly 60 knots as they stream down the leeward slopes. Colorado is known, for example, for its Chinook winds that are akin to the Santa Anas of Southern California. As winds stream downhill, they heat due to compression and temperatures in Denver could rise as much as 50-degrees Fahrenheit very quickly. Pilots need to recognize and respect the conditions that favor such dramatic wind patterns and be wary of downdrafts on the lee side of mountain ridges.

Viewers were made aware of turbulent conditions, exacerbated by high temperatures, instability, and gusty winds, that could, at their worst, result in loss of control and, at their least, make it risky to cross mountain ridges at midday in the summer. And every potential mountain pilot who viewed the film heard the warning, "Beware Density Altitude."

Accident reports filed with the FAA and with the National Transportation Safety Board (NTSB) have been rife with mishaps that, upon study, revealed inadequate knowledge on the part of pilots. It can be risky for the uninitiated to attempt to fly in mountainous terrain, to take off or land at airports at altitudes of 6,000 or 8,000 feet, or to press on into inclement weather conditions in aircraft that are unable to respond quickly and to perform well at high altitudes. Craggy peaks can reach skyward higher than the ceiling above which some aircraft can climb. The movie emphasized the common sense of learning from an instructor pilot like Emily who has been well experienced in mountain flying. News reports rarely boasted about safe flying and pleasant and successful flights; news reports focused on the incidents, the accidents, the fatal crashes that engendered ghastly headlines and attracted media attention and sales.

Bold, big headlines cried, "Aircraft Overdue, Pilot and Two Children Presumed Lost;" "Wreckage of Light Aircraft Strewn in Narrow Ravine," or "Airplane Found at 10,000 feet, No Survivors." Reports stated, "...and the single engine aircraft is believed to be down in rugged, inaccessible country. Ground search is hampered by continuing icing conditions and poor visibility;" "...the twin-engined private plane on a flight plan from Texas to Aspen, Colorado has disappeared. Heavy snow and below zero temperatures threaten the lives of possible survivors."

Clearly, in the interest of air safety, instruction about flight in mountainous terrain was necessary and the FAA wanted that material disseminated as widely as possible. Emily was contacted by the FAA and she, in turn, contacted one of her flight students, Jerry McGuire, to see whether he wanted to participate in the scripted, directed film.

While McGuire had taken his flight lessons with Emily, he'd taped the sessions in preparation for a book that they would co-author. In *Learning How To Fly An Airplane*, he wrote that he responded to the invitation with, "Me? Fly all day for free? You bet!"

Importantly, McGuire had not yet tried any mountain flying, so his selection as inexperienced student pilot was apt. The FAA producer, Stephan Dobert, and an independent film director, Jerry Ward, prepared the story line and set up two aircraft for the filming. As the subject aircraft, Dobert and Ward chose a Cessna Cardinal RG, a retractable geared Cardinal with fully cantilevered wings that presented a sleek, attractive craft and enhanced the movie.

Emily knew the Rocky Mountains intimately, as a camper, a horseback rider, a wife, mother, and pilot. A natural to star in the FAA film, "Mountain Flying," she had hiked, ridden, and flown repeatedly in mountainous terrain, sharing them with Stanley.

McGuire had no previous experience in flying an aircraft equipped with retractable gear. It made sense to Emily that Jerry first be acquainted with the airplane before attempting the mountain flying and the formation flying necessary for filming. They got that check out of the way—all thirty minutes of it—and McGuire was given the story line for his first casting as a movie star. Dobert told him, "You've just flown to Denver with your family, landed, and have parked your airplane. When the line boy asks you where you're headed, you respond, 'West.' The line boy will suggest that you get an introduction to mountain flying with an instructor pilot familiar with its unique qualities."

Air-to-air footage was shot from a Cessna 210 camera plane that had the right door removed. It was piloted by the FAA's Bruce Romick and bore two cameramen, Ward and Bill Schwartz. Jerry McGuire and Emily planned their route of flight and he filed a flight plan from Denver's Arapahoe County Airport to the high elevation airfield at Granby. Filming started right away with the flight planning scene, shots of the preflight check of the Cardinal, and, with Emily sitting in the right seat to teach the student who was accustomed to her instruction, filming the aircraft departing to experience flight over the Rocky Mountains. McGuire said, "That was enough realism to qualify the whole program for a TV adventure series or maybe a situation comedy."

Emily told McGuire to climb to reach 10,000 feet prior to reaching the foothills, a 5,000-foot gain in altitude. She identified peaks that created Corona Pass, letting him know that their course would take them between those peaks at 14,000 feet. She also informed him that he was legal to fly at that altitude without oxygen for no longer than 30 minutes. She emphasized that identifiable peaks are a help, but stressed the importance of keeping track of your whereabouts in the mountains. He noticed that mountains that surrounded an aircraft could confuse directions unless attention was given to pilotage, map reading, and consulting the instruments. This is exacerbated by deteriorating visibility due to rain, clouds, smoke, or hazy conditions.

Emily had required Jerry to get a forecast of the winds aloft prior to departure, but, as they neared the Pass, she urged that he get an update from the Flight Service Station. When told that the winds would be from the west at 23 knots, Emily told him, "If the winds are greater than 30 to 35, forget the flight. Go another way or another day."

"As you climb out of 10,000 feet," she continued, "you can figure that you've lost about half of your horsepower. Your airplane will perform much more sluggishly than it does at sea level."

Emily taught him to take advantage of ridge lift to gain altitude, and then instructed that, to cross the ridge, he approach it at a 45-degree angle. This enables a pilot to veer toward lower terrain if any downdraft suddenly erases altitude gains. Made aware of the term Density Altitude in ground school and in preparation for written tests, Jerry learned first hand about the reduced performance of the Cardinal as he and Emily performed takeoffs and landings for the film crew at Granby, elevation 8,203. An aircraft can get airborne at high altitude on a hot day when there is high humidity, but it may not be able to climb out of ground effect (the cushion of air that exists within one wingspan of the ground) and be able to avoid the obstacles that could be telephone poles and wires, tall trees, or, much more permanently, granite hidden in the clouds.

Lessons learned? Emily taught all of her students: "Remember High, Hot, and Humid" and plan your mountain flying for early morning or quiet evening when the temperatures drop and the air is less turbulent. Properly preflight making certain that weather briefings and winds aloft are part of your knowledge base. Remember that the topography and circulation of air results in air rising on the windward side and tumbling or sliding more rapidly down the leeward side. Learn the signposts: clouds that denote stable conditions (stratus) might also signal poor visibility, clouds that indicate instability (cumulus) warn of updrafts and downdrafts and, when darkening and boiling upward, warn of possible thunderstorm activity. Give any mountain thunderstorm wide berth. Give yourself at least 1,500- to 2,000-feet of clearance when crossing ridges and cross them at 45-degree angles. Know your limitations and know your abilities. Although it was downplayed in the FAA movie, she taught students to carry survival kits and jugs of water when flying into the Rockies. She was never a fearful pilot. She was a prepared pilot and she taught her students by setting a good example.

When Jerry McGuire completed his flight training, he and Emily went on to publish their book with Tab Books, Pennsylvania. He wrote, "…Emily, of course, has had more to do with my enjoyment of flying than anyone. She's the kind of instructor every student pilot ought to have because she is serious about flying and she demands concentration, preparation, and the [proper] execution of every detail between the pre-flight check and locking the doors when the lesson has been completed. While I will never understand how any flight instructor can remain calm during a lesson, Emily always appeared to be at ease when I was at the controls. That helps a student build confidence, which is extremely important. …To me, most of my training was a delightful experience, but not all of it. There were plenty of times when I was sweating, uncomfortable, scared, too slow or fast, high or low. Calmly and gently, Emily kicked my rear and insisted that I get it right. I couldn't have become a pilot without her help and experience." McGuire speaks for literally hundreds of students who learned what they knew from Emily.

Emily and Stanley with the airplanes they both enjoyed.

Trying to Fly the Line

Throughout the 1960s, Emily had followed the hiring swings of United Air Lines, Continental Air Lines, and Frontier—the three which, were she lucky enough to be hired, would offer a chance for her to stay in Denver—and she resolutely submitted applications for employment. She already knew that she was more experienced at flying than many of her students. Yet, she was told, repeatedly, "The airlines aren't hiring women."

From the days of the Suffragettes working tirelessly for the right to vote for women and for black citizens, the economic and social destinies of blacks and women had been linked. Emily had known of the Civil Rights Act of 1964, had heard the first faint rumblings of women's push for equality, for "equal pay for equal work," but she had not heard of Perry H. Young, Junior, the first black pilot hired as a commercial pilot. Receiving only rejection in the United

States, Young was forced to gain his flight experience during a decade in Haiti, Puerto Rico, and the U.S. Virgin Islands. Despite an excellent record as an instructor for the pilots of the famed Tuskegee Airmen during World War II— he taught more than 150 young men everything that they know about flying— no aviation jobs were open to him in the United States.

In December 1956, ten years after having earned his first pilot's license in Ohio and having flown fixed-wing and rotary-wing craft in the Caribbean, Mr. Young was hired by New York Airways in an aggressive campaign to break the color barrier in the commercial airlines. Young rose to captain within months and flew with the company for 23 years—from 1957 until 1979.

An article in the New York Times stated, "After Mr. Young was hired by New York Airways, other men became emboldened to challenge the status quo. Marlon Green, a former Air Force captain, took Continental Air Lines all the way to the Supreme Court in 1963, winning a landmark judgment that opened interstate commercial airlines to black pilots."

Marlon Green was hired in Denver, Colorado. Emily knew of Green's challenge and knew that, as an Air Force pilot, he had the necessary qualifications and flight experience to take to the cockpit of airliners. She respected Green, identified with the deep frustrations that he must have felt, and understood his need to forcibly open doors when his Air Force background clearly demonstrated his capability. The airlines sought pilots who had been trained by the military; unfortunately, that search hadn't included black military pilots and it had included no women pilots. Black pilot Mildred Carter, trained at Tuskegee under the Civilian Pilot Training Program, was turned down when she applied to fly with the Women Airforce Service Pilots. After World War II, WASP pilot and Mercury 13 pilot Irene Leverton brought military flight training and a wealth of flying experience to her applications for a crew position with the airlines. She, too, faced rejection.

As ushered in with the Civil Rights Act, taking employers to court had become a viable option and one avenue open to those who faced bias and discrimination in their jobs and careers. In order to be the first in her field and to command the salary of an airline pilot, Emily could have resorted to law courts. She could have raised angry demands for her rightful place in the cockpits of commercial airlines. The idea was suggested to her.

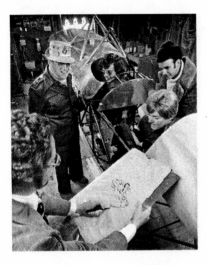

Some of Emily's supporters, calling themselves the Skybats, fitted her into the cockpit of their experimental Steens Skybolt while it was under construction. Pete Finicle is in the front cockpit, on the right is Don Davila, center is UAL's Ed Mack Miller, and, the caricaturist, is Pat Oliphant.

A good friend, Ed Mack Miller, was a senior captain with United Air Lines who wrote a column on aviation in Denver and hosted a radio talk show on which he interviewed memorable Denver citizens. In the mid-sixties, Emily, then a flight instructor who had made obvious her desire to be flying the line, was invited by Miller to be a guest on his talk show. Miller mentioned on the show that Marlon Green had been hired by Continental Air Lines. He commented, "You know? It's about time for a woman to be hired. You might even have a lawsuit that would be in your favor."

Emily protested sincerely, "I don't want to do that. I want to be hired for my own merits. I don't have the training and the experience in the military that Marlon Green has. I can understand that the airlines want military pilots; few are as well-trained as they. But, it could make the working conditions unbearable were I to force my way in. I bet that I'd face nothing but resentment and fury from the captains and crew members who were scheduled to fly with me."

Ed Miller respected her position. He believed that she would be an asset as an airline pilot and he wrote a letter of recommendation for Emily.

Emily took Stanley flying often, posing here to advertise Clinton's aerobatic course. Note the upside down "Learn to Fly Me" on the fuselage.

Chief Pilot

When Jim Muncey left his employ with Lou Clinton, Emily was next in line to become the Chief Pilot of Clinton Aviation. This brought her added responsibility, as she not only saw to it that the fixed base operation met all the requirements of a Federal Aviation Regulations Part 141 flight school and the aircraft charter business under Part 135, but she became the check pilot and FAA designated flight test pilot for graduating pilot applicants: private, commercial, instrument, flight instructor, flight instructor instrument, single- and multi-engine land.

She said, "It was a great opportunity. As usual, there was more to learn than I'd anticipated and the challenge was stimulating. On the downside, however, the job demanded so much in the way of management that I didn't get chances to fly as often as I had become accustomed to and as often as I would have liked.

"At the same time, too, I was 30 years old and sincerely afraid that my age would further keep me out of an airline cockpit as my gender was already managing to do. I coveted the salary earned by airline pilots, wanting to do the best that I could for Stanley and to see to it that he could one day obtain the college education that I was never afforded. I didn't see a great future in General Aviation and I hated the thought that I could be denied an airline piloting job because I am a woman and because I was rapidly becoming too old."

Emily often represented Clinton Aviation promoting flying via static displays with aircraft, taking prospective students and journalists for introductory flights, or, as in this image, addressing service groups in the Denver metropolitan area.

Emily quietly positioned herself where she could not be ignored, she resolutely obtained the qualifications that were required, and she conducted her professional flying with standards of excellence that couldn't be denied or refuted. She doubled her flight hours, thanks to the United Air Lines Contract Instrument Training Program. She obtained more multi-engine flying time and earned the highest rating available to pilots—the Airline Transport Pilot (ATP), first for single-engine and later for multi-engine aircraft. She continued to submit applications to Frontier, Continental, and United.

"Frontier is Hiring"

In September 1972, John Bata, a flight instructor who had worked for Emily at Clinton Aviation, reported that he'd just had a successful airline interview.

"Frontier Airlines is hiring, Emily. They're looking for pilots."

Soon thereafter John was hired and Emily's desire to be the first woman at the controls of an airliner in the United States became almost overwhelming. All she could think was, "Oh, I don't want this opportunity to go by!"

Emily, Chief Pilot at Clinton Aviation, taught instrument flying to male pilots already hired to fly as airline pilots for two full years. Despite her flight experience, she was denied the opportunity to become an airline pilot until Frontier Airlines felt the breath of the winds of change. Frontier selected the best woman for the job. The rest is history.

Connie Bowlin, Delta Air Lines Captain, Warbird pilot, and Author, wrote, "In 1973, I was learning to fly. To fly an airplane, any airplane, was a dream come true. Then a lady named Emily Howell was hired by Frontier Airlines and I realized that my dream could be even bigger. ...Maybe, I could someday become an Air Line Pilot.

"Following in Emily's footsteps as one of the first 50 women hired by a U.S. airline, I realized, just as Emily did, that we had an opportunity to set an example and to encourage others to pursue a career in aviation. Whether I am flying as Captain on a Boeing 767 or flying old World War II Fighters or Bombers or a J-3 cub, I know there are a lot of people who would love to do what I do and what Emily has done. It wasn't always smooth sailing for Emily, with the "ups and downs" of the airline industry, but she continued doing what she loved and I know you will enjoy and be encouraged by her story! Good Luck to all of you who are pursuing your dreams and Thank You, Emily!"

CHAPTER 5: "NO" ISN'T AN ACCEPTABLE ANSWER

"Nothing in the world can take the place of persistence.
Talent will not; nothing is more common than unsuccessful men with talent.
Genius will not; unrewarded genius is almost a proverb.
Education alone will not; the world is full of educated derelicts.
Persistence and determination alone are omnipotent." *Calvin Coolidge*

Early in 1970, when Emily applied for a flight officer position with Frontier Airlines, she had over 5,000 flight hours to her credit. Johnny Meyer of the Training Department told her, "The airline is not hiring."

She updated an application that had been filed with Continental Air Lines from September 1969 to September 1970 and addressed it to the wife of Continental's president, Mrs. Robert F. Six, the popular screen star Audrey Meadows. Emily wrote, in part, "I'm certified to give flight tests for private, commercial, instrument, and multi-engine in a Cessna 310, Cessna 320, and Cessna 337, which is the Skymaster with centerline thrust. I hold air taxi certificates for the C-310 and C-421 for charter under Part 135 [of the Federal Aviation Administration Regulations]. I am a designated Aviation Safety Counselor with the FAA and I currently have logged 5,500 flight hours."

Meadows responded by writing, "I've received your résumé and all the interesting facts about your marvelous career. I've discussed this information with Mr. Six and we have routed your file to Mr. Red Stubben, Continental's Vice President, Flight Operations, for his review and consideration. He will be in touch with you regarding this matter. Wishing you every success, Sincerely, Mrs. Robert F. Six."

It was a gentle rejection; but, it was one more rejection.

In 1971, she reapplied to Frontier and was told by Frontier's Administrator for Employment and Safety that her application would be kept on file for the period of one year. He added that hiring might be possible by spring of 1973 and that her application and qualifications would be considered.

In 1972, reapplying to Continental, she went to visit Mr. Dan Purse, Continental's Personnel Director. Initially he told her, "We will keep you informed."

Then, Emily became more assertive. She recalled, "Bonnie Tiburzi's photo appeared in Ladies Home Journal as an aspiring pilot. I'd seen that and it seemed to be writing on the wall. It made me all the more eager. All I could think was that 'I'm not the only one out there waiting for the chance!' I told Dan that I just knew that some airline was going to hire a woman one of these days.

"He said, 'I wish it could be us.' I wanted to say, 'Why don't you make it Continental?' all the while wishing that he could make it happen. I hadn't realized how important it was to me to become an airline pilot. All I could think was, 'I've come this far, I've tried since 1967. I really want the job!'"

Frontier was Hiring

By September 1972, Emily had greatly extended her network of friends. John Bata was one of those who made a difference for her. As soon as she heard Bata's assertion, "Frontier's hiring," she rushed to the offices of Frontier Airlines that very afternoon.

"I was excited; however, I was also angry. I'd just given a fellow a multiengine flight test and he'd done a terrible job. He was already hired by Frontier and I knew I could fly better than he. It rankled that a pilot like that already had a job with the airlines and I couldn't even be considered. I headed for Frontier's offices."

The Personnel Office, open between 9 a.m. and noon, was closed. Initially, Emily was terribly disappointed, but it turned out for the best. Forced to take more time, her temper cooled and she was able to better prepare herself and become more professional in her approach.

She researched all the applications she had ever submitted, analyzing to update all pertinent information and taking until midnight to rewrite carefully. She appeared at the Personnel Office the next morning with two crisp copies—one addressed to the Personnel Office and a second, also neatly packaged, for Johnny Meyer, still the Chief Pilot.

When the female receptionist asked what her application was for and was told that she wanted a pilot position, she asked, "Pilot? How many hours do you have?"

Emily amazed her by answering, "I have 7,000."

She repeated, "Really? Will you wait a minute?"

She entered the inner office and brought a man out with her, saying, "…and she has 7,000 hours!"

The man accepted Emily's application and agreed to deliver one to Johnny Meyer.

A few days later, Bob Wilson, who had also been a Clinton Flight Instructor and who'd been hired by Frontier in 1967, telephoned to say, teasingly, "Hey, Emily, Andy Hoschock, the chief interviewer of all new applicants at Frontier, asked me about you when he found out that I knew you. I told him that you fly pretty well, …for a girl."

Then he continued more seriously, "I told him that I'd known you a long time and that you have a good reputation in aviation circles. I told him that you've taught Frontier and United airline pilots how to fly and that you are a good instructor."

Emily thanked him sincerely and urged, "Keep the word going around, will you? If you hear anything, please give me a call."

What would she have done without supportive friends? Networking was key to being considered for a job and to getting an interview. Former students mentioned her name and, fortuitously, a Convair 580 simulator instructor, Ken Contratti, invited her to watch the simulator in action. Ed Mack Miller wrote a letter on her behalf to Frontier's Ed O'Neil, Vice President of Flight Operations, sending Emily a copy of the letter, which stated, in part, "…Ed, you'd better hire this gal. You're going to miss the boat if you don't. I want to hear from you on this."

Emily began regularly scheduled visits to the front offices every two weeks, getting on first name basis with everyone that she met. Two other loyal friends for whom she was grateful were Roy Williams and Jack Gardner.

On 5 January 1973, Gardner called to say, "Frontier is in the process of hiring another class. I was in the meeting when your name was mentioned. They dropped it like a hot potato. They didn't want to touch it."

Emily's heart sank. "Have you any suggestions, Jack? What should I do?"

"Get your tail over here this afternoon. I'll meet you at the coffee machines at 3 o'clock. I haven't figured it all out yet, but I'll get you in to see Ed O'Neil."

Scheduled to give an Instrument Check Ride that afternoon, Emily had flown with the pilot, Doc Eagin, and knew him to be competent. She bent the rules a bit and said, "Flight plan a short ride. You'll get your instrument rating if you avoid making a single mistake. We'll fly between Arapahoe County Airport and Denver's Stapleton. Show me a perfect ILS approach to Runway 35 at Stapleton and the rating is yours."

Emily admitted, "It was probably the shortest instrument check ride in history. We took off, leveled at 7,000 feet, asked for and got a clearance for an ILS approach, and landed. We were airborne all of 15 minutes and, despite the brevity, he did a great job and earned an instrument rating. Later, he gave me justification—he became an airline pilot.

"While the instrument applicant waited for me, I went to Frontier's offices and met Jack Gardner. He said, 'I'm headed for the reception area outside of

Ed O'Neil's office. You just walk in a bit behind me and I'll take it from there.'"

Emily waited five minutes and, when she entered, Jack turned to ask, "Emily! What are you doing here?"

"I'm hoping to see Mr. O'Neil."

"We can do that. Come on with me."

He opened O'Neil's door, looked in, and said, "Ed, I'd like to interrupt you for a moment. I've got somebody here to see you."

Ed, a gruff, but gentlemanly Irishman, asked, "Oh? Well, who's that?"

"Emily Howell. She wants to talk to you."

Emily could hear his voice change a bit, becoming a bit edgy; but, he invited them in.

Jack ushered her in, suggested that she sit down, and said, as he turned to leave, "Why don't you two talk?"

Facing the most important salesmanship of her life, Emily had to sell herself to someone who wasn't very interested in buying.

After giving her almost three quarters of an hour of his time, Ed O'Neil told her, "Well, we'll be in touch with you."

Those words weren't new to Emily, but she left as graciously as she could.

The next day a staff member from the personnel office did call her. She was invited back for another interview with Ed O'Neil that afternoon. She said, "That was my first invitation for an interview and I could scarcely contain my excitement. I'm sure it reflected in my voice, 'Certainly I can be over there!' My heart beat loud enough for everyone in the office to hear."

When Emily arrived, dressed tastefully in a tailored suit, Andy Hoschock cooperated in the interview with Ed O'Neil. One of their questions was, "You have a son, don't you?"

When she answered in the affirmative, he asked, "How would you handle his care?"

66

There have been later interviewees who have responded to such a question with a curt, "Do you ask that of your male applicants?"

But that wasn't Emily's style. She was ecstatic to be in the interview and strove to make careful, cogent responses. She told them of her supportive family and explained that her mother was willing to care for Stanley if she were to be away.

Andy asked, "What would we do for a uniform for you?" and Emily insisted, "Well, pants suits are in. I'll go to a tailor and have a uniform similar to the male uniforms styled to fit me."

She couldn't help but think that that was the least of their worries.

Andy warned, "You'd be leaving a lucrative position as Chief Pilot for Clinton. You'd be taking a pay cut to fly for Frontier."

Emily agreed, "That's true, Captain Hoschock, but I'll be gaining something else."

"What's that?"

"A seniority number!"

He acknowledged that as a good point and cracked the slightest of smiles.

This was a tough interview. They didn't want to hire her and they put up every obstacle that came to mind. Emily responded firmly and patiently. She finally suggested, "Wouldn't Frontier's President like to get in on this?"

Frontier's President was Alvin Lindbergh Feldman, an engineer from Akron, Ohio. Feldman was an employee of Aerojet General Corporation, which, in turn, was a subsidiary of General Tire and Rubber Company, the holder of a controlling interest in Frontier Airlines. Feldman was sent to Denver in 1971, ostensibly to close the airline. He instead opted to strengthen Frontier and see it succeed, choosing as one approach to involve every employee in either sales or operations. Taking on the novelty of hiring the first woman as one of his operations personnel would have been viewed as an interesting challenge for this dynamic man.

Having already spoken with President Feldman, O'Neil agreed and said, "This is as good a time as any for you to meet him."

The trio went upstairs and Al Feldman was very direct. He asked a lot of questions and then he did something that impressed Emily greatly. He excused himself to telephone his wife with the news that Emily was in his office.

His wife, Rose Emily Feldman, was a pacesetter. An engineer like her husband, Mrs. Feldman's previous employer had been aviation's Convair Corporation. Feldman held his wife in high esteem and it was to Emily's good fortune that he had a healthy respect for women's achievements. To judge from his one-sided conversation with his wife, she was encouraging about Emily's application and interview. Emily was truly grateful.

One of the questions raised was Emily's strength in handling an aircraft like the Convair 580. Truthfully, she told them, "I would think that I can handle the controls, but I don't really know as I've never flown that airplane." Andy Hoschock and Ed O'Neil discussed with Mr. Feldman the idea of getting Emily into the Convair 580 simulator. They placated her with, '...just to see what you think of it. This won't be a test.'"

Emily, relieved that she had been given the time to observe CV 580 simulator rides, made a mental note to thank Ken Contratti.

To the question, "How about if it is available right now?" Emily assured them, "Certainly," sounding a great deal more confident than she felt.

The sim was occupied, but, invited to return at six o'clock in the evening, Emily left with a cyclone of mixed emotions spinning in her head. "How can I arrange to be at my best in the sim? Who could give me some pointers immediately? This is the biggest opportunity of my life. I can't blow it now!"

Doc Eagin and Emily flew back to Clinton and Emily immediately called two friends, Bob Wilson and Jack Howell, the first an instructor at Clinton and the second a Captain with Frontier. Jack, despite his name was no relation and was also one of her multiengine instructors who trained her toward her Airline

68

Transport Pilot rating (ATP). He knew her well. She begged for a short course on flying the Convair 580 simulator, telling them that her chance to fly it was only a few short hours away.

Both men were encouraging and Jack suggested that she review the Navy Basic Instrument Flying handbook. She knew that intense pressure could be counter-productive, but knew that any pointers from more experienced pilots would give her added confidence. It was to her credit that she had given so much instrument instruction to United Air Lines' trainees and, like a mantra, she repeated to herself, Remember the basics—climbs, glides, turns, approaches, departures, and level flight! Concentrate on the basics.

That January evening was dark and cold when Emily drove to Frontier's offices. Word had spread about her chance to fly the simulator. The receptionist to whom she'd given her application said, "We're rooting for you."

Emily's adrenaline reached fever pitch. When Ed O'Neil arrived, they strode briskly down a long hall to the simulator. Jack Robins, who joined them as they entered a room that bore an enlarged image of Convair 580 instrument panels, asked, "Do you want to know anything about some of these?"

"You could tell me about some of the gauges," Emily told him.

She heard little of what he said. She could see his mouth moving and knew that he was trying to be helpful; but, feeling the anticipation and angst that most pilots feel prior to a challenging task, all she could think was, "Get me through this. Oh, Lord, get me through this. Just let me get into the sim and get started. Once we're simulating flying, everything will start to fall into place."

Given the chance for questions, she asked, "Who's going to fly in the left seat? Mr. O'Neil, are you going to be in the left seat?"

Ed looked a bit stunned. He hadn't been in the left seat of any aircraft for perhaps five years. As Vice President of Flight Operations, his flying was sporadic.

Jack urged, "Ed, that's a great idea. You get into the left seat and I'll be behind you. I'll run the flight." Neither man mentioned the words, "check ride." They didn't have to.

Ed climbed into the Pilot-In-Command (PIC) position and Emily sat in the right seat. In the 580 sim, the windshield was covered and flying was done relating solely to the instruments, although the pressures on the controls were realistic.

They fired up the engines and gradually got "airborne." Thinking that the 580 was going to be very heavy on the controls, she rotated too much on the initial takeoff. But she could begin to feel the ship and grow accustomed to its required input. They did some gentle turns, some steep turns, a couple of stalls, and then they shot some approaches. They gave Emily vectors to headings and requested some altitude changes. As she worked the sim, she recognized that the simulator "flew" like a Cessna 310. Experienced in that twin-engined aircraft, her confidence grew.

Before landing, Emily heard, "We'll give you an engine failure on takeoff now. That creates a little more stress on the airplane."

She knew that it would try to turn on her and readied herself for application of a rudder pedal, depending upon which engine was failed. They cut the engine at V_1 (the air speed at which an aircraft can maintain forward flight with one engine inoperative) and Emily kept the nose straight, but failed to use sufficient back pressure to establish a shallow climb. She admitted her mistake and asked if she could try again.

Ed O'Neil assured her that they could try as many times as she wanted. But, it only took one more try. The second time she was quicker to use the correct procedures. The airplane responded, climbing, one engine out. Once handling familiar controls, her experience took over. She knew what she was doing. She also knew that the men would love to see her fail. Her resolve stiffened.

They flew the simulated landing pattern, shot a single-engine approach, and, readily admitting that she wasn't familiar with their landing procedures, what was expected in the way of radio transmissions or call-outs in the event of emergency procedures or during normal operations, she received some help on the airline SOPs (standard operating procedures).

After they'd been in the simulator for a couple of hours, Jack Robins asked Emily how she was doing. In reality, she was close to exhaustion, even her voice was giving out; but, she managed a cheerful, "I'm just fine."

Jack said that they could do some more and Emily responded, "I'm ready for whatever you want."

"Aw, we've had enough," was his response.

The post-flight briefing was held at a long table with Ed at one end, Jack in the middle, and Emily seated at the other end. Jack started painting a discouraging picture of the realities facing an airline pilot. He said, "You'd be flying long days. The weather can be horrendous. Sometimes you can expect to shoot as many as five approaches in blowing snow or driving rain in a single day. It can be grueling and exhausting. You'll be away from your home a great deal. There are times you'll have uncomfortable flight pairings. With low seniority, your bids will result in you getting the shaft. If you fail to bid, you might get unbid blocks and those schedules can be rotten." He finished with, "Have you ever thought of selling real estate or something?"

Ed pulled a book from a nearby table and showed it to Emily. It was Robert Serling's *She'll Never Get Off the Ground*. Published in 1971, Emily had read it and understood the implication. Anti-discrimination laws were newly coming into effect. The Civil Rights Act, which had precipitated a number of lawsuits, had caused major corporation CEOs to re-evaluate their policies and to assiduously avoid arbitrary discrimination against women and other minorities. The fictional young woman of Serling's story, though special in her flight skills and determined to enter and succeed in a man's world, was accused of flaunting the safety of her passengers when, in Serling's fiction, her sole motivation was emotional. The novel pitted her choice to save the life of the man she loved over the safety of her passengers and called it a "feminine emotionalism."

"What do you think, Emily?" Ed asked, "Someone just gave me this book. Do you think I should read it?"

Emily knew that they were trying to rid themselves of her like one swats a pesky mosquito. She wanted to say, "Do you suppose emotion can be attributed only to women?" Aloud, she said, "I wouldn't bother with it, if I were you. It doesn't have a very worthwhile ending." She smiled and added, "There is only one thing that fictional pilot and I have in common. We both drive Mustangs."

The mood lightened just a bit. Then, seriously and quietly, Emily said, "I want to be an airline pilot. I would really like a flying job with Frontier Airlines. Mr. O'Neil, I want this job. I know I'm capable of doing it and doing it well."

The change in the man was barely perceptible. His shoulders sagged ever so slightly and his jaw tightened. Then, he said, "All right, Emily. But, I want you to think about three things when you go home. ..."

Ed leaned forward on his forearms. "Will this job be good for you?" He paused. "Will you be good for Frontier Airlines?" He paused again. "Will your hiring as a Frontier pilot be good for other women involved in aviation?"

He stood slowly up and added, "I'll wait to hear from you in the morning."

Emily could scarcely feel the floor under her feet as she left. "The job is mine! How incredible!"

On 17 January 1973, Emily joined Frontier Airlines as a pilot. Her introductory training began on 29 January 1973 and she flew as a Second Officer aboard a Boeing 737 jet for her first flight on 6 February 1973. Outfitted with a uniform, now displayed at the Smithsonian's National Air & Space Museum, Emily entered the previously all-male bastion, the cockpit. She knew that she was the right woman for the job; now she had a chance to prove it.

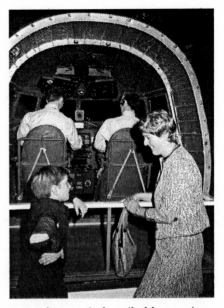

Emily lets Stanley get a glimpse of a simulator – a Convair 580 simulator tested her competence as a pilot and modern CAE full motion simulators figured prominently in her career with the FAA.

Persistence and Determination

Aviation historians discover one tale after another that reflect the determination that sparked the careers of pioneer aviators. Our earliest mentors were not discouraged by the frailties of their flimsy machines, their lack of complete understanding of aerodynamics, unpredictable and inclement weather, or indescribable reactions to what we know today to be hypoxia, vertigo, and/or carbon monoxide poisoning. Those who took to the sky exhibited indomitable spirit and dogged persistence.

Such qualities were needed especially among the women who became pilots—those who overcame not only the daunting challenges of flight, but also the prejudice and discrimination that faced their entry into what had been exclusively a man's world. Nowhere was this more apparent than in the cockpits of commercial airlines.

On 17 January 1973, Emily refused to take "No" for an answer. She took introductory training and, climbing aboard a B-737 to fly as Second Officer with Captain Swede Nettleblad and First Officer Vern Tidwell on 6 February, became the first woman crewmember to pilot a scheduled U.S. jet airliner.

Now her work was cut out for her. Now she had to fly the line and fly it well. Her story was about to take off.

On her first flight as a crew member, 6 February 1973, Emily and one of the flight attendants posed on the steps of Frontier Airlines' Boeing 737 in which Emily was about to make history. This uniform of Emily's is now on permanent display at the prestigious National Air & Space Museum, Smithsonian.

CHAPTER 6: A FIRST FRONTIER FOR A WOMAN

Airlines in the United States made their debut in 1914 as pilots Roger and Tony Jannus flew an open cockpit Benoist Airboat as an aerial taxi between Tampa and St. Petersburg, Florida. This initial commercial endeavor carried one passenger at a time and flew 18 miles in approximately 25 minutes; the flight carved an hour and a half off the length of a boat trip and an amazing 11 and a half hours from the same trip by rail. This represented a humble start to what has grown into an intricate global service that includes a multiplicity of national and independent aircraft carrying millions of travelers.

Natural obstacles like lakes, channels, and rivers that prevented or slowed travel by rail or road were incentives to aerial transportation. However, lacking a large body of water to be traversed, like the English Channel that gave impetus to airline creation in England and France, commercial aviation was slow to take root in the United States. It wasn't until attention was turned to carrying the mail by air that airline service came to the fore; thus, our nation's commercial transportation was born of a necessity to speed written communication, not for the purpose of transporting people. When transcontinental air mail became a reality, the air transportation of U.S. citizens was underway.

A political step in the creation of the private U.S. airline industry was the 1925 Contract Air Mail Act. Those who captured the first contracts were: National Air Transport, Varney Air Lines, Western Air Express, Colonial Air Transport, and Robertson Aircraft Corporation. The first two later figured importantly in United Air Lines. In a merger, Western and Transcontinental Air Transport later became Transcontinental and Western Air (TWA). Robertson, Colonial, Southern Air Transport, and others became American Airways. Pioneering international air travel was Pan American (PanAm), which was founded in 1927, and Pitcairn Aviation became Eastern Air Transport, later Eastern Airlines.

To emphasize one difficulty in tracing U.S. airlines, one large aircraft designed and created by Alfred Lawson in 1919 was piloted on one round-trip from Milwaukee, Wisconsin to New York City, on to Washington, DC, and back toward Milwaukee. The craft landed near Dayton, Ohio where it was forced to undergo repairs prior to completing the journey to Wisconsin. Emblazoned on its fuselage was "Lawson Air Line;" but, there was one Lawson airliner and no Lawson air line.

The Roaring Twenties

In 1925, Dwight Morrow, the father of Anne, the famed author and the first U.S. woman to obtain a glider license who later married the celebrated aviator Charles Lindbergh, had been a senior partner with J.P. Morgan when he was tapped by then U.S. President Calvin Coolidge, to chair a board that would establish a national aviation policy. The results of Morrow's board became the Air Commerce Act of 1926. In a sweeping move, this act designated airman, airwoman, and aircraft licensing; aerial navigation methods, routes, and air accident investigation. What began as private industry swept into the realm of governmental regulatory control.

In 1927, Ford Motor Company tycoon, Henry Ford, produced the three-engined cargo and passenger plane and Charles Lindbergh soloed his Ryan across the Atlantic Ocean. Aviation and aviators became heroic in scope; "Lucky Lindy" captured the hearts of the nation's citizens and the air excited everyone's imagination. The previously unbelievable concept that people would be carried across the earth's oceans was altered forever. Airline travel would become the preeminent form of transportation. In the ensuing 76 years, many airlines have emerged; some have succeeded and grown, some have merged and united, and others have failed like meteors shooting brilliantly and briefly across a night sky.

The Thirties

By 1934, as the United States slowly began its climb out of the devastation of The Depression, a scandal had surrounded the letting of airmail contracts and routes. Giving the task to military pilots seemed a solution; however, accidents beleaguered the temporary takeover of airmail delivery by the U.S. Army. A solution was sought in the passage of an Air Mail Act. This Act, in part, resulted in a more even distribution of the government mail contracts; this, in turn, spotlighted the need for aircraft to be designed that would place emphasis on passengers. Passengers had avoided transportation by air, seeking their travel arrangements via the more familiar railroad lines. Travel by air began to attract passengers when safe delivery of the mail began to impress the public.

By 1938, the airlines were placed under a central agency, the Civil Aeronautics Authority. This agency, with the authority to regulate airmail rates, airline tariffs, routes, mergers, and agreements between lines, was intended to protect the long-term interests of the airlines and to promote stability for mail delivery and for passenger carriage in the industry. Between the CAA, the later FAA, and the rapid technological advances in materials, manufacturing processes, and design, the airlines grew concomitantly with improvements in aircraft. Advancements made in military aviation were shared with the commercial airlines and the necessity to enter World War II and respond to German and Japanese aggressions resulted in rapid changes in civilian aircraft when the war was over.

Emily had the good fortune to meet two famous pioneering women pilots of the Thirties and the Forties, Kay Menges Brick and Blanche Noyes.

Frontier Airlines

Frontier Airlines came into existence in Denver, Colorado on 1 June 1950 with the merger of three carriers, Arizona Airways, Challenger Airlines, and Monarch Airlines. Arizona Airways had started in the spring of 1946 as an intrastate line serving Phoenix, specializing in scenic tours of natural grandeur like that of the Grand Canyon. Issued a certificate in 1948 by the CAB, Arizona Airways held a contract for carrying airmail and at the time of the merger owned three DC-3s. Challenger Airlines, which offered its four DC-3s to the merger, had started as Summit Airways, a corporation organized in December 1941 in Wyoming. Granted a certificate in 1946 by the CAB to operate air carrier service from Billings to Salt Lake City, the company became Challenger Airlines in 1947. Based after 1947 in Salt Lake City, Challenger purchased two more DC-3s and served Utah, Wyoming, and Colorado. It moved its headquarters to Denver in 1948 and, during the blizzard of 1949, lived up to its name by flying thousands of passengers and tons of food and supplies. In Denver, Challenger shared maintenance and sales with Monarch Airlines, which had started scheduled service in 1946 between Denver and Durango, and then Albuquerque, Salt Lake City, and Grand Junction.

Interestingly, Monarch's weather operations were pioneered by having installed its own navigational system. Monarch, bringing its five DC-3s, bought controlling interest in Challenger in 1949.

Paul Hainey, a friend and colleague with whom she later worked in the FAA, was Captain in the Boeing 737 to Emily's First Officer position, Frontier Airlines.

Frontier Airlines existed between 1950 to the end of August 1986, thirteen years after Emily's hire, when it was purchased by People Express, which absorbed its routes and equipment and held onto the airline for only three or four months. Emily was forced to apply for unemployment benefits. By 1 February 1987, however, Continental Air Lines had taken over Frontier, People Express, and New York Air, becoming the third largest U.S. airline. Whereas People Express had its eye on Frontier's equipment and its routes, Continental absorbed many of its crewmembers, including Emily. She learned first hand the disruption caused by mergers, the loss of seniority position, and the threat to holding the prestigious role of Captain.

Eight years after Frontier closed its doors, the current Frontier Airlines initiated operations on 5 July 1994. This rebirth came about with the advent of a new and enlarged airport in Denver, the downsizing of some Denver operations by other airlines that left availability for the start-up of a "new" airline, and the capability of the airline to take advantage of several executives who had been employed by the Frontier Airlines that had been willing, in 1973, to hire the first woman pilot.

Emily's refusal to take "no" for an answer from Frontier indicated a persistence and determination that were not unique to Emily, but were two of her strongest assets. One Frontier Captain with whom she flew, Billy Walker, said this of Emily's crucial interview with Frontier's Ed O'Neil and her capabilities, "During the 12 years Emily spent flying as an instructor pilot, she trained numerous students who went on to various airlines. This irony was not lost on Emily. She taught these students and helped them progress into the airline cockpits where she strived to be.

"Frontier Airlines' Vice President of Operations Ed O'Neil recognized Emily's potential and needed only to confirm her airmanship and strength of character. Even if she could fly, she would have to endure the discrimination sure to exist in the male dominated atmosphere of the airliner flight deck. Through a lengthy interview, Ed, as with everyone who knew Emily, discovered she was probably the best candidate available to handle the bias. Now, he needed to see if she could handle the controls of one of the most difficult airliners to hand fly that was in use in the early 1970s.

"The Convair 580 was a very powerful twin turbine powered aircraft that was extremely heavy on the controls. It had been converted from piston power to turbine power in the early 1960s, allowing the 44 passenger seats to be expanded to 53, the gross weight to be increased by approximately 10,000 pounds, and the speed increased by 100 MPH. The original CV-340/440, originally designed as a turbo-prop but introduced with piston power, could barely maintain 9,500 feet of altitude on one engine.

"The conversion to turbine power produced an awesome improvement in performance and utility. The 580 could lose the critical engine at take-off on a hot day at a high altitude airport, climb to 10,000 feet, and cruise faster on the remaining engine than its 340/440 predecessor could go with both engines running well. One drawback to the conversion was in flight control response. The CV-240/340/440 control response was light, while the 580 flight controls were very heavy. Pilots used to remark they had to work out with weights for six months to be strong enough to fly the 580. Others claimed there were heel marks on the lower instrument panel where pilots had to brace themselves in order to pull back on the control column for takeoff rotation—exaggerations, for sure, but they point out that Emily, as a female, should have had trouble flying the Convair 580.

"...The Convair 580 simulator was sophisticated for its time. It was able to replicate the feel and sounds of the aircraft and the cockpit display of the simulator was identical to that of the aircraft. Although motion was absent, flying the 580 simulator was still very real. The test was to see if Emily could handle the stiff controls and she had her work cut out for her. She was highly competent in light aircraft but had zero experience in large aircraft. Due to her unique position, she would be asked to demonstrate much more than her male counterparts would be called upon to do in a pre-employment sim check. Being first does not come without its cost. She knew that, if she were to fail, she would not be the only woman affected. She knew her failure would reflect upon all women."

Airline Pilot Qualifications

What were some requirements for any pilot to be considered, male or female? When Emily was hired, few pilots over the age of 32 were considered. She was correct in assuming that she could have been summarily dismissed on the grounds that she was too old to be hired. Secondly, Emily did not possess a college education. Fortunately and fairly, all of the education that she achieved in training for FAA written tests, FAA flight tests, conducting flight and ground school courses, and in being the educator who tested applicants for their flight certificates and ratings, she more than indicated that she held the equivalency of any college degree. Yet, this might have been an insurmountable obstacle and a ready way for Ed O'Neil to toss Emily's application into the trash. Thirdly, an airline pilot must meet high standards in physical health. Here Emily's confidence was well placed as she had consecutively passed FAA medical examinations every year in order to maintain her position as a Certificated Flight Instructor. In addition, she displayed the qualities of good judgment and a good attitude that aid and abet a crew position that requires mutual accommodation and respect.

Jet Powered Flight

Military jets first appeared in the skies in aerial battles over Europe during World War II. The German Messerschmitt Me 262, like a blazing skyrocket, displayed speed that challenged the pilots of piston-driven craft. The first commercial jet, the British de Havilland Comet, made dramatic strides as a prototype, but two fatal crashes spotlighted design characteristics that needed to be addressed and corrected to offer passenger and crew safety. Boeing Corporation jumped into the jet age that had been introduced in Britain and, when it unveiled its 707, PanAm ordered 20 on 13 October 1955 and ordered 25 Douglas DC-8s, as well. The jet age in commercial airlines blazed into being. By 1969, it surged with the entry of widebody and supersonic jets; PanAm again led the field with the first purchase of the Boeing 747.

In 1958, the Federal Aviation Act resulted in the formation of the Federal Aviation Agency, now the Federal Aviation Administration (FAA), a safety regulatory agency. It had never even crossed Emily's mind that, as she was submitting applications during the 1960s to United, Continental, and Frontier, she not only would fly for the two latter airlines, but she would complete her career in aviation in the FAA. Nor did she have an inkling that her first flight with Frontier would be in a Boeing 737 and that her retirement in 2002 would be from the position of Air Crew Manager for United Air Lines' Boeing 737-300/500 fleet. She said, "I had to laugh. I flew my first flight in the jump seat as a third pilot and, as an Air Crew Manager, guess where I rode? There I was—right back in the very same jump seat position."

On 6 February 1973, television and radio reporters gather to cover Emily's historic first flight in the Boeing 737 – the first U.S. woman pilot in modern airline service.

First Frontier Flight as a Pilot

When Emily climbed into that jump seat to fly as 2nd Officer aboard a Frontier Airlines' B-737 on 6 February 1973, the route of flight was from Denver to Las Vegas, back to Denver, and then on to St. Louis and return. Each leg would last approximately one hour, forty minutes and each pilot would have his, and now her, duties.

Before she could even get started, she received a call from a local newscaster, Bob Howard, who said, "Emily, I want the scoop here. I want to break this story! I've heard something; is it true?" Emily told him that she'd let him know and that she would call him first.

Jim Ramsey, a member of Frontier's Public Relations Department, called to say that the phones had rung off the wall; callers had been full of questions.

The PR folks set up a press release and a press briefing; they arranged for her to be in the hangar at 2 p.m. with an airplane, Mr. O'Neil, and invited members of the press. The official announcement was to be issued.

Emily said, "I called Bob Howard and told him to go ahead and break the story. He was a flight student at the time and was jubilant to get the scoop."

Then it came time for her first flight. Captain Swede Nettleblad and First Officer Vern Tidwell had been specifically selected for Emily's history-making appearance. Both could be counted on to be patient with the media frenzy surrounding the flight as well as with the unique concept of sharing their cockpit with a woman. As the trio approached to enter the crew room, newspapermen and cameramen swarmed around the terminal at Stapleton.

"It was a relief to enter the crew room," said Emily. "But I knew I'd face popping flashbulbs when I started toward the plane and at each destination, Vegas, St. Louis, and especially in Denver.

"In the crew room, the Captain organized all the paperwork, including: actual and forecast weather, a flight release, flight plan, and any Notices to Airmen (NOTAMS) that pertained to the route of flight. I was to be the third flying officer aboard and Swede asked me to do the preflight check. Wind, rain, snow, whatever, the first officer is out there. People tease by saying, 'Kicking the tires, lighting the fires,' but actually the walk around is important for ensuring visually that the aircraft is ready for flight, the tires have the proper inflation, and there are no discrepancies that might hamper a safe flight. Everything looked okay to me, so I went back into the cockpit. Swede and Vern were testing the fire system to ensure that it was working, obtaining our fuel and our weight and balance releases, and checking the batteries for voltage (normally between 24 to 30 volts in the 737). The Captain followed the 'flow pattern,' starting on the left side of the cockpit and checking all the switches, setting them as desired, and checking the clock. The First Officer had a similar flow pattern and, although mine was more limited in items to check, I followed a flow pattern, too. A fuel pump was turned on and, using an Auxiliary Power Unit (APU) that is internal to the aircraft, the generators were brought on line, the engines were started, and my first taxi was soon to be underway.

"As second officer, I was sitting in the Flight Engineer's position, so I had nothing to do with the aircraft control in that flight; but, luckily I had a lot to think about or my excitement might have gotten out of hand. The radio panel was just above my head and my oxygen was over to the right. I was thrilled; but, knowing that I was in the spotlight and that my every move would be scrutinized, I focused on my job.

"In those days, being Second Officer on a B-737 was like the fireman's position on a train. It was a seat that the FAA regulated, a center seat between the two pilots. It could be pulled down for seating and I was positioned looking forward; but, a second officer was not necessary to the flight. Later, in eliminating the position, the duties of Second Officers were simply added to the First Officer's load. I was charged with taking care of the company radio, getting briefings on the weather, and taking care of the passengers' comfort with the heat and air conditioning. I was also responsible for written reports— the time sheets, the logbooks, and any noted discrepancies that the Captain wanted written for maintenance follow-up. It was important that the time sheets be accurate and the fact that they became the pay record added incentive to their accuracy. Of course, I was also charged with anything else that the captain called for or expected. But, the most important thing was that I was given a seniority number; I was there as part of the crew. I was happy!

"Forewarned that there would be a lot of publicity associated with the flight, Swede and Vern were great about it. Cameramen even called up from the ramp to have me open a window in the cockpit and lean out with a wave. It was all such a new experience; I didn't have any idea of how to open a Boeing jet's window.

"I felt as if I were a goldfish. It was embarrassing to have the media following me, all eyes on me. It was awkward. I felt as if the other pilots were thinking, 'Oh, brother!' I felt as if everyone else was on the outside and I was in a bowl that enlarged and exaggerated my every move."

The B-737-200 carries 97 passengers and the flight was close to full capacity for Emily's breakthrough flight. Even the passengers were queried by persistent reporters who wanted to know how they felt to know there was a woman pilot aboard. Even though it was Emily's sincere desire to be an airline pilot and to perform at her very best in that position, there was an awareness throughout the day—in Denver, in Las Vegas, back in Denver, in St. Louis, and, at the end of the day, home in Denver—that an historic first had occurred and that a new frontier for women pilots had been surpassed. How prophetic the name of the airline!

Attention paid to this historic first didn't end with Emily's initial flight. Soon thereafter, she received a large congratulatory bouquet of flowers all beautifully decorated in red, white, and blue from the Scandinavian airline pilot who had so inspired her, Turi Wideroe.

Among other appearances, Emily was flown to New York City to be interviewed by Ed Newman on The Today Show and her son, Stanley, went with her when she was a participant on the show, What's My Line? Later, Emily and Stanley did a television commercial for the orange drink, "Tang." In one auspicious event three years after she was hired, Emily was invited to Washington, DC, escorted by Colorado Representative Gary Hart, to speak in a program celebrating International Women's Year. Again, Stanley, who was escorted by Colorado Representative Pat Shroeder, went along, dressed in a little tuxedo.

At home in Colorado, Emily and Stanley loved spending time in the mountains. Owning horses was just one of their pleasures. Their Granby home is located near the headwaters of the Colorado River.

Emily said, "Here was my son, perched between two politicians. He looked so cute. Stanley was seven when I was hired. He was old enough to know what was going on and he got involved in some of the interviews and some of the publicity. I think it was exciting for him; it made him a bit of a celebrity at school. Of course, Frontier Airlines reaped some publicity, too. It was up to me to ensure that the coverage was positive!"

On Emily's second flight, the temperature in the cockpit had dropped to below freezing. Upon arrival to fly, she reached out to extend her hand and the Captain said, brusquely, "I don't shake hands." A bit later, when they were about to depart, he turned to her and spoke the only seven words that he uttered on the flight. He said, "Don't touch a thing on this airplane."

Emily came into her position carrying a soft stick. She managed, as good leaders do, to develop camaraderie and respect by demonstrating her own piloting skills and keeping her own counsel. She recognized that everything she did, every move she made was forming the reputation that could make or break her in her position. She said, "You build your reputation over a long time."

She complied with the Captain's demand, patiently holding her tongue and folding her hands in her lap; but, at the end of the flight, she followed him onto the crew bus. Although there were plenty of empty seats, she chose to sit directly next to him. When the bus stopped at the terminal, she stood up, said, "I enjoyed flying with you, Captain. Good night." He grumbled a reply, and then gradually, over time, accepted that Emily was on the line to stay.

Right from the first flight, Emily received a seniority number, which insured that she could move ahead. Within six months, she was offered a bid to fly as First Officer on the Twin Otter. It wasn't long after that that the Air Line Pilots Association (ALPA) voted out the position of Second Officer on the Boeing 737. Frontier Airlines was among the first to do away with the position, the ALPA Council in Frontier agreeing with the ruling.

Emily said, "Some other airlines weren't too happy with Frontier because it meant a loss of a lot of jobs. But Frontier protected people who could no longer fill a piloting position. They were put into different jobs until spaces opened up and allowed them back to fly the line."

Parenting

At home in Denver, Emily and Stanley moved to live in a condominium located adjacent to Emily's brother Dennis' and his wife Jeane's home. Dennis, a contractor, created a connecting doorway between Stanley's bedroom and his children's room, enabling Stanley to sleep in his own bed every night. Jeane, who was a stay-at-home-mom, was always available to take care of Stanley if Emily or if Emily's mother was not there. Stanley walked to the elementary school that he attended, although, soon after having started grammar school, his teachers recommended that he receive counseling because of his hyperactivity and difficulties in concentrating. It was recommended that he be moved to a school that had smaller numbers of children in the classes.

Emily bought a little house on 17th Avenue because it was near St. Elizabeth's School that boasted only approximately 20 children per class. Stanley was tested medically and the doctor felt that he might be a candidate for Ritalin. Trying to avoid that, Emily learned that Children's Hospital was opening a program for children with learning disabilities. She said, "I applied for that and put Stanley through testing for the program. He received all sorts of comprehension tests and was interviewed and evaluated. He was found to have a learning disability and attention disorder, but neither was severe enough to enroll him into the main program. He was on the fringe. I was forced to think about the doctor's recommendation of Ritalin."

Stan Howell, Emily's first husband, is shown with his two sons. In front of him is Garrett and on the right is his and Emily's son and his namesake, Stanley, with whom he shared a close relationship.

Flying the Twin Otter

In 1951, de Havilland produced a single-engined land- and sea-plane that proved itself as a workhorse. Over 450 were built and were flown in search and rescue, as carriers for paratroopers, for aerial photography, and widespread commercial use. That popular aircraft was lengthened by ten feet, its wingspan increased by seven feet, and hung with two Pratt & Whitney turboprop engines that increased its speed by 50 miles per hour, and the DHC-6 Twin Otter first flew in 1965. It had accommodations for two pilots and between 13 and 20 passengers or up to 4,280 pounds of freight.

Emily got her first bid, a job opening as first officer, in Great Falls, Montana on 4 August 1973. A pilot who had flown as a flight instructor at Clinton Aviation and was hired by Frontier was already based with his wife and family in Great Falls. Invited to live with them and assured that Stanley would be cared for when Emily was away on trips, she and Stanley moved to Great Falls and set up a basement apartment in their home.

"I received my training in the actual airplane and then, very early one morning, the telephone rang. My check airman, no relation, was Jack Howell. He was calling to notify me that I was going to receive my Initial Operating Experience (IOE), a check ride, and that I had to be at the airport at 5:30 that morning. I felt as if I'd just gotten into bed and I gasped, '5:30? I just got in!'

Jack brushed it off with a, 'Aw, you can handle it. See you at the airport.'

I called a taxi and jumped in his cab, heading up the bluff to Great Falls Airport. On the way, I was really wired. I babbled to the driver, telling him all about it and how proud I was to be going where I was going."

The check was grueling. Emily said, "We flew from Great Falls, straight north to Glendive, Montana, and then across the northern tier, to Sidney, Montana, to Williston, North Dakota, then down to Rapid City, South Dakota. We ate lunch in Rapid City, and headed back to Great Falls. It was a ten-hour day and a full eight hours of flying. During the rest of that summer, whenever the load on the Twin Otter was light, my host, who had a son Stanley's age, suggested that we take the boys with us for the day. Stanley got a big kick out of those flights."

Incidents Also Fly the Line

Emily admitted that one of the dumber mistakes that she made was to "Cancel IFR" during an airline leg. To Cancel IFR meant to let the controllers know that you are no longer going to operate under the rules of instrument flying. In General Aviation and in good weather conditions, it makes sense to "Cancel IFR" when it represents having the terrain in clear view, taking over visually for the remainder of the flight, and letting down in visual contact to bypass the extensions of flying an instrument approach. She explained, "I was a Captain, flying a 737 from Kalispell to Missoula, Montana. In the approach to Missoula, there are several hills and valleys. The weather was gorgeous, so I decided to take over visually and the tower controller in Missoula told us to call on final over the marker.

"I responded, 'Roger,' and added, 'we're out of 12,000,' and I began the descent. I was heading directly toward where I thought the airport was and I called for the first officer to lower the gear. All of a sudden it occurred to me that I couldn't find the airport. 'Shit. I'm in the wrong valley!'

"I poured the coals to it and told the first officer, 'I just made a big mistake here; we're not descending where we should be.'

"I pulled up, called gear up and, when I was high enough to call the tower, heard the controller say, 'We've been trying to transmit to you. Where are you?'

"I said, 'We're just coming up on the marker now.' They never knew, thank goodness. When we got on the ground, the flight attendant asked, 'Hey, Emily, did you put the gear down for some reason before we were ready to land?'

"'I was just checking it for proper engagement...'"

There have been others who have flown into the wrong airport. El Paso, Texas and Biggs Army Air Field have two similarly long runways that, due to the prevailing winds, replicate each other exactly and are less than five miles apart. In clear weather, both stand out. In inclement weather, mistakes have been made.

Emily recalled that a crew from Frontier landed at an airport north of Salt Lake City when they were headed for Salt Lake. They compounded the error by taking off again. She said, "First of all, don't land at the wrong airport. But, if you DO, don't take OFF! If the field is not normally a destination airport for the airline, there will be no published performance requirements for the aircraft: weight bearing capacity of the runway, runway length, landing weight of the aircraft, departure weight of the aircraft, fuel load, number of passengers, and so forth. You're in trouble having landed, but, upon taking off again, the trouble increases exponentially. Letters start arriving from the FAA and the captain has many questions to answer.

Back to Denver

"When a job opened in Denver for a Twin Otter pilot, I bid on that and got it. Stanley and I moved back to Denver and I flew as first officer in the DHC-6 out of Stapleton until the fall of 1974. When a bid opened for the Convair 580, I jumped into that. I went into training and flew the Convair until about 1976.

"Then an opening for Captain on the Twin Otter came up; I bid in a heartbeat. It was my first Captain's bid and it proved to be a really good experience for me."

Life couldn't have been much better for Emily than in 1976. She upgraded to Captain on 9 June and took the coveted left seat. Best of all, Emily had met a prospective pilot at Clinton Aviation in 1967. Julius "Jay" Warner, who had been enrolled in the U.S. Navy pre-flight training program, had not set foot in an airplane when World War II came to an end and the program ended. After having taken advantage of obtaining his college degree and motivated to pursue flight training, he signed up for lessons at Clinton Aviation. He became one of Emily's star pupils.

She said, "Jay was a natural. I soloed him in six hours. Later, as he progressed, we would have a flight lesson and then he would take me to lunch. We've been going to lunch together off and on ever since."

Having fallen deeply in love, Emily became Mrs. Jay Warner on 18 November 1976. In a happy union that brought an extended family together, Stanley added three stepsisters, Julia, Elizabeth, and Susie, and two stepbrothers, John and David, to his life. Already close to Theresa and Neil, he grew close to Susie, partly because they were close in age and partly because they shared the home with Emily and Jay.

Emily and Julius "Jay" Warner enjoy the Colorado skies in their Cessna 182.

A Captain Takes Control

When Emily had been 18 years old and in flight training with Jim Muncey, she was having the time of her life. It was Munce who finally impressed upon her that flying was fun, but that she needed to treat flying seriously, too. He warned her that she had to get ready to fly solo. At the time, Emily hadn't realized that she would take an airplane out by herself. When she went through her introductory flight, she heard about the hours she needed to fly and the price of flying per hour, but she didn't take into account some of the flying that would be expected of her.

She said, "I thought about soloing an airplane and, boy, it was as if a line had been drawn. I was challenged. Right then and there I went from having nothing but fun to taking it seriously. That is how flying has hit me ever since. I had to assume responsibility. It was a lesson that I've never forgotten."

Later, when Emily told Jim Muncey that she wanted to be a flight instructor, she said, "I want to teach people to fly." He responded, "Nope." When she asked what he meant, he said, "You want to teach people to fly safely." That was a second lesson that she never forgot. Important to general aviation, to the airlines, to military piloting, and to flight in space, safety is the most important consideration. She admitted, "I concentrate on safety, but I still have a lot of fun. When it isn't fun anymore, it will be the time to quit."

Becoming the first woman pilot to become an airline Captain was another historic first. Emily said, "When you get the left seat is important to your career. The experience of command and leadership is vital. It was a great move for me at the time. The responsibility that I'd learned to assume as a student pilot and the emphasis on safety were absolutely essential now."

Astronaut and then-Director of the Smithsonian's National Air & Space Museum Michael Collins wrote to invite Emily to be the first to donate a women's airline uniform for display. Emily and Stanley traveled together to the nation's capitol in 1977 to see her uniform to its new and prestigious location. They enjoyed touring NASM as well as giving Stanley the opportunity to see the museums, the monuments, and the architectural beauty that Washington boasts. It was a very special treat for them both.

In 1977, Emily took Stanley for a tour of
Washington, DC when her uniform was installed
on display at the Smithsonian's
National Air & Space Museum.

On becoming a Captain, an airline pilot moves from the right seat in the cockpit, the First Officer position, to the left seat. The captain bears responsibility for the safety of the passengers, crew, and cargo for each flight under his or her control. The Second Officer, in aircraft that require three crewmembers, assists with the flight and must be duly certified as a pilot, although the Second Officer position is focused upon the mechanical and electronic devices of the aircraft. Emily started in the Second Officer position; however, the First Officer is a starting position in those aircraft that do not or no longer require a third crew member. An airline pilot receives a seniority number. That number only is hampered in the event of the merger or sale or closure of the airline of employ. Emily was the first U.S. woman pilot to become a captain—with Frontier in the DHC-6 Twin Otter.

CHAPTER 7: ON BEING FIRST

Airliners in the United States took to the skies as soon as dreamers could convince citizens of the safety and comfort of aerial transportation. The first airline pilots were almost exclusively male. In 1973, Emily Howell Warner shattered that pattern and changed its direction – for her own aviation career and for the professional careers of all women who followed in her footsteps.

How do we establish "firsts" in aviation history? And, having once acknowledged those significant and historic facts, isn't it more productive to focus on the benefit that has been achieved by one and extended to many?

Some aviation "firsts," like the record-setting flights sanctioned by the National Aeronautical Association (NAA), are well documented, officially observed, and irrefutable. Others are clouded by terminology and the rapid changes that characterized powered flight during aviation's dynamic first century.

To establish Emily Warner's legitimate claim as the first woman hired to pilot an airliner in the modern U. S. scheduled jet airlines, one has to explore the history of those airlines and the women pilots who contributed to that history. Although Emily's story has been well documented in magazine articles and news reports, some contradiction and competition to Emily's position reared with the publishing in 1984 of *TAKEOFF, The Story of America's First Woman Pilot for a Major Airline* by Bonnie Tiburzi and Valerie Moolman. American Airlines' pilot Bonnie Tiburzi's story, which reached the bookshelves eleven years after Emily had been hired, stole a bit of Emily's thunder.

Like the competitive space flights of pioneers Yuri Gagarin and Alan Shepard, which occurred within weeks of one another, the airline careers of Emily Warner and Bonnie Tiburzi began only a matter of months apart. Emily, by 5 January 1973 and with 7,000 flying hours logged, had finally obtained a long-sought interview with Frontier Airlines and was hired as a flight crew member. Her first orientation training started on 29 January and Emily took her first history making flight in a Boeing 737 on 6 February. Tiburzi, in late February and with 1,400 flight hours logged, reported to Dallas-Fort Worth Airport to be interviewed for a piloting position with American Airlines. Her career took wing within three months of that initial interview.

Emily Howell and Bonnie Tiburzi, the first two women hired as pilots for the U.S. Airlines.

In her book, Tiburzi reports having heard of a few pioneering women pilots, but having no contemporary woman pilot to whom to look as an example. Emily said about her flight training days in 1958-59, "There were some women in the Denver flight school when I was learning to fly. We became good friends; they shared what I was going through. But, there were several women pilots who made an impression on me. Soon after I started taking flying lessons, I had the chance to meet the pioneer pilot, Ruth Nichols, who was in Denver signing her autobiography, *Wings For Life*. Nichols noted that she had been certificated as a pilot by the Fédération Aéronautique Internationale (FAI) in 1924, the 19th woman licensed in United States, and that she was, in her time, the only woman to have held three international records for altitude, speed, and long distance. It was an honor to meet her. She autographed her book for me, writing, 'To Emily Hanrahan, Best wishes on her own flying career.'

"Then, attending my first meeting of The Ninety-Nines, the International Organization of Woman Pilots, really brought home to me what women were capable of doing and what they had done in the past. I was honored to be introduced to some WASPs [members of the Women Airforce Service Pilots], among them Betty Jo Reed, Grace Birge Mayfield, and the fixed-wing and helicopter pilot, Betty Pfister. That was wonderful! I met Gene Nora Jessen, the International President of The Ninety-Nines and one of the outstanding woman pilots who had undergone and passed the same tests that were given to the U.S. astronauts in the NASA Mercury space program. She helped me a great deal. Gene Nora, a member of the Oklahoma City Chapter, was visiting The Ninety-Nines Section Meeting in Denver. When I discovered that she was a flight instructor at Oklahoma State University, I remember saying, 'A flight instructor!' I was in awe."

In 1961, the same year that Emily earned her flight instructor rating, she read a newspaper account of the hiring of Turi Wideroe as the first female pilot to fly for Scandinavian Air Lines (SAS). She was delighted and inspired to read of the Norwegian woman at the controls of an airliner. When Emily's hiring by Frontier Airlines was broadcast to the world, one of the first persons to send a note of congratulations and a bouquet of flowers—tastefully arranged in the patriotic colors of red, white, and blue—was Turi Wideroe. Emily pressed the flowers, cherishing the note.

As in every field of endeavor, women who later sought careers are appreciative of those who were trailblazers for us all. In the U.S. military services, the WASP, including the WAFS, were the first U.S. women to pilot the arsenal of military aircraft. In air transportation, Emily was the first to open the cockpit doors. Those of us who have followed and have pursued a wide variety of aviation careers owe debts of gratitude to the talents and persistence of Emily, Bonnie Tiburzi, and the many others who quickly followed. They were hired on their merits and in the belief that they could perform safely and well in careers that previously were held by male pilots.

Women Pilots, Members of ISA +21 meet in Denver in 1980. Emily Warner, a Charter Member, is 4th from the bottom on the right. Photo Courtesy of ISA +21

Thanks in part to the changing societal attitudes in "The Sixties" and to the Civil Rights Act of 1964 that focused attention on the equal treatment of candidates in the work force, opportunities beckoned. As a highly qualified pilot, one who had trained many male pilots for airline careers, Emily took her rightful place as the first. Her hiring rightly changed the emphasis from a gender issue to one of competence and capability.

Soon after Emily was hired, other women took to airliner cockpits. In 1978, professional women airline pilots united in the International Society of Women Airline Pilots (ISA + 21). With Beverly Bass and Stephanie Wallach as Founding Members, the Charter Members are: Denise Blankinship, Jane Bonny, Julie Clark, Gail Gorski, Jean Harper, Mary Horton, Claudia Jones Sorenson, Karen Kahn, Sharon Krask, Angela Masson, Holly Mullins, Norah O'Neill, Lynn Rhoades, Terry Rinehart, Margaret Rose, Lennie Sorenson, Sandra Szigeti, Valerie Walker, and Emily Howell Warner. Their achievements are a matter of record.

Airline Certification

In *Takeoff!* Tiburzi wrote, "I picked up an airline magazine on the homebound plane [from her first interview with American Airlines]. ...In it was a little squib of a story about Emily Howell having been hired by Frontier Airlines as a flight crew member ...There was also mention of a Barbara Barrett flying for Zantop, a small Michigan regional that apparently spent a lot of its time going in and out of business. ...Maybe I do have a chance in the majors."

The term Major Airlines did not come into common use until 1980, after the Airline Deregulation Act of 1978 and seven years after Emily was hired by Frontier. United States' airline history made its modest beginning with one two-seater flying boat that transported paying customers across Tampa Bay in Florida in 1914. For most of the 1920s, surface transportation was more comfortable, more reliable, and more popular than air travel. It was well into the 1930s, following the dramatic ocean crossing of Charles Lindbergh in 1927, that the traveling public began to become air-minded and to seek increasingly

101

safe, efficient, and speedy forms of aerial transportation. Aircraft began to be recognized as the trains and boats of the skies.

By 1963, the U.S. certificated scheduled airlines were classified as Domestic Trunks, Local Service and Helicopter lines, Intra-Alaskan and Intra-Hawaiian lines, and All-Cargo and U.S. International and Territorial lines. When Emily was hired in 1973, she was hired by a U.S. certificated scheduled airline, a Domestic Trunk. Tiburzi, too, was hired by a Domestic Trunk.

Five years later, after the Airline Deregulation Act of 1978, the list changed to identify 11 Trunks and 26 Local or Regional airlines. Within some of the larger states – Hawaii, Alaska, California, and Texas – Intra-State airlines operated and, nationally, there were Cargo Carriers, Commuter Airlines, and Non-Scheduled Airlines – the "non-scheds" – that been denied authority by the Civil Aeronautics Board (CAB) to operate scheduled routes.

Deregulation in 1978 created enormous upheaval and resembled a feeding frenzy among saltwater fish, the larger rapidly gulping down the smaller. Large airlines became larger and several of the Trunks disappeared completely. Of the 26 Regionals, one survived – USAir – and grew to become a Trunk. Intra-state lines reached beyond their state borders, yet only one – Southwest Airlines – survived. Cargo carriers did not escape the changes wrought by deregulation and Commuter lines, also swallowed up by larger lines, were absorbed outright or joined forces with specific trunk lines. The larger Non-Scheds – like World, Transamerica, and Capitol – forged scheduled routes and then found it impossible to continue. World survived, but returned to its non-scheduled status.

After deregulation, classifications changed as well. By 1980, Trunks became the newly designated Major Airlines and the Regionals became the Nationals. With Alaska Airlines, the remaining airlines dominated commercial air transport in the United States.

Modern Major Airlines were those airlines earning revenues of $1 billion or more annually in scheduled service. Able to provide national and international service, in 1996 the twelve major U.S. airlines—Alaska, American, America West, Continental, Delta, Federal Express, Northwest, Southwest, TWA, United, UPS, and US Airways—were classified according to revenue rather than according to the carriage of cargo, passengers, or both.

Pilot Certification

The certification of pilots progressed through a similar series of name changes. Were women hired to pilot airliners? Then, as now, the nomenclature is important in designating those who came first.

The U.S. Government first certificated pilots in 1926 and enforced certification as a requirement. Prior to that, pilots were unlicensed or were licensed under the auspices of the Aero Club of America or by the Fédération Aéronautique Internationale. These licenses were not required, but were sought by pilots for recognition of their demonstrated flying abilities.

The early designation for those pilots who could be paid for carrying passengers in aircraft was the Transport License. Later, this certificate, with added requirements, was renamed the Commercial License. As pilots began training, they obtained Student Pilot Certificates. Those enabled them to fly with flight instructors, fly solo over supervised and designated routes, and amass solo flying hours toward the Private Pilot Certificate. With a Private license, a pilot could fly alone over unrestricted routes and was permitted to carry passengers, but not for hire. To carry passengers for hire, a pilot had to obtain more than 200 hours of flying time, pass a written and a flight test for Commercial Pilot, and, for the safety of passengers, be hired to operate under Parts 121 or 135 of the Federal Aviation Regulations.

Confusion arises with the designation of airlines as Commercial Aviation. There is a distinction between a Commercial pilot—one who has earned a

Commercial Certificate—and a pilot of a Scheduled Commercial Airline—currently required to have earned an Airline Transport Pilot Rating, the ATP or the ATR.

Which women were among the first? In 1928, Edith Foltz Stearns flew approximately 100 flying hours as a co-pilot on a tri-motor Bach aircraft that was used on the West Coast Air Transport, an air service, between Seattle and San Francisco. In 1930, Elizabeth Russell joined the flying staff of the Royle and Andrews Flying Service at Alameda, California. At 18, she was touted as having been one of the youngest commercial pilots in the country. Ruth Nichols, whom Emily was proud to have met, flew as a pilot for New York and New England Airways in 1932. Each of these were designated as air services, technically not the equivalent of a scheduled airline, although this in no way demeans the accomplishments and the contributions of these capable pilots.

In December of 1934, Helen Richey was hired as the first woman in the United States to take to the controls of an airliner. At that time, Central Airlines, which carried mail, was in bitter competition with Pennsylvania Airlines and Helen's position with the airline was designed to create a great deal of positive publicity. Helen believed that she had received a sincere offer and that she would demonstrate her ability and, thus, the ability of women fliers. Flying seven airline flights in January 1935, Helen then began to be phased out of the cockpit. During the spring and summer of 1935, she flew less than a dozen trips while male co-pilots flew ten times as many. Her historic place in U.S. commercial aviation is secure, but it was devastatingly depressing to Helen. Although she had set numerous flying records, had served admirably in the U.S. government's airmarking campaign, and had flown during WWII for the British Air Transport Auxiliary (ATA) and as a member of the U.S. Women Airforce Service Pilots (WASP), Helen was denied a flying career after the war.

On 7 January 1947, she took her own life. She was 38 years old and tragically, despite having made major aviation achievements, she was born too soon.

Frontier Airlines, a U.S. Scheduled Airline offering jet service, hired Emily Howell Warner in January 1973—an historic first for women pilots. Unlike the hiring of Helen Richey and despite the fact that Frontier Airlines reaped a great deal of publicity, Emily was not hired for public relations nor was she hired on a temporary basis. She was hired to work as a pilot, to keep the same schedule as male pilots, and to do so for an extended period of time. She took her first flights toward an illustrious career in aviation and has not swerved from that goal.

The first in her family to take an airplane flight, Emily was the first in her family to consider taking flying lessons. Fortunately, no one ever told her that she couldn't weave the winds of chance, the winds of change, and the winds of opportunity to pursue her dreams.

CHAPTER 8: ISA +21 and A FIRST FOR ALPA

Emily's hiring broke through the barricades; more women moved rapidly into the void, each aspiring to become the airline pilot that Emily demonstrated women were capable of becoming. By the end of her year of hire, 1973, four women pilots were flying for the U.S. airlines. That number doubled by the end of 1974, tripled by the end of 1975, and, by the end of 1976, there were 22 women flying the U.S. lines.

Frontier Hires First Woman Pilot In U.S.

Frontier News published this headline shortly after Emily's hire.

Lori Cline, a gifted U.S. woman pilot, pocketed her private certificate in 1979, six years after Emily was hired. By 1981, she had graduated from Indiana State University with certification in: Commercial, Instrument, Multiengine, Multiengine Instructor, Instrument Instructor, Seaplane, Glider, and Helicopter. She was hired by Atlantis Airlines, a commuter service based in South Carolina. Too young to have earned her ATP (age 23 was required for eligibility); Lori flew for Atlantis, qualifying for an ATP with an age waiver, but passed over for Captain nine times as her seniority rose. On her 23rd birthday, 1983, she waited in the FAA office for an official to erase her waiver and sign her ATP certificate. That afternoon, Lori flew as the youngest woman airline captain in the world.

Like Emily, Lori is interested in inspiring young women to pursue aviation and aerospace careers. In one memorable moment, she occupied the left seat of her Piedmont Airlines' Boeing 737/200 when a male passenger brought his daughter, aged eight, past the cockpit as they entered the craft. The daughter said, "Daddy, can I be a pilot when I grow up?"

The man patted his daughter's head and said, "Oh, no, honey. You could never do that." Lori invited the child into the first officer's seat, took some time to tell her about flying an airliner, and let her know that, if she truly wanted to become a pilot, there was no reason she should let that dream go.

Lori also recalled helping an elderly woman board her Atlantis flight. Before going to her own first officer's position, she stowed the woman's suitcase and helped her fasten her safety belt. After they landed, Lori stepped out of the cockpit to greet the departing passengers. The old woman smiled at Lori and said, "How nice of the captain to let you sit right up front."

These encounters happened years ago, yet, even today, ISA +21, the International Society of Women Airline Pilots to which Emily and Lori belong, has the dual challenge of encouraging women to think of airline careers and to educate the public about women rightfully and competently taking their places in the cockpits of airliners.

Women pilot members of ISA +21 gather for the 1983 conference. Emily celebrated her tenth year as an airline pilot. She is second from the right in the rear. *Photo courtesy of ISA +21*

About ISA, Lori wrote, "The women [newly taking their airline cockpit seats] quickly settled into their routines in the male-dominated environment, but couldn't help but wonder how the women at the other airlines were faring. Often they would spot one another in the terminal buildings or in a crew bus and secretly long to have the chance to get acquainted. There were so many questions to ask: Had they encountered the same challenges with training and ground school? ...Each thought, 'What an opportunity it would be to meet and share ideas and experiences.'"

At a dinner together in 1977, Beverley Bass of American Airlines and Stephanie Wallach of Braniff Air Lines discussed the possibility of bringing together the women who were flying for U.S. carriers. When Beverley and Stephanie approached a few more, Claudia Jones, a Continental Air Lines pilot, offered to arrange for an initial get-together in Las Vegas, Nevada. The invitations went out and all women airline pilots were invited to congregate in May of 1978.

Emily joined the twenty-one women from ten U.S. air carriers who were in attendance at what turned out to be the start of a vital and important organization. The International Social Affiliation of Women Airline Pilots sprouted quickly from that planted seed and, now known as the International Society of Women Airline Pilots, it continues to flourish.

The Charter Members at that historic first meeting could recognize that, for most of them, their tension-filled probation period was over. Probation lasted for the first year of employment and represented the year in which an airline can terminate the contract if performance doesn't meet the airline's expectations. They spent much of the convention simply getting acquainted and sharing experiences, discussing the pros and cons of creating a political as well as social organization. Most believed that they were well represented by their respective airline unions and opted to have theirs focus on a social organization.

Choosing an aviation acronym, their name—ISA +21—echoes the familiar ISA that aviators recognize as the Standard Temperature Aloft. (In aviation, ISA +21 indicates a temperature aloft that is 21-degrees higher than standard.) They added a Plus 21 to recognize those in attendance at the first conference and therefore those who chartered and charted the organization. A similar precedent was set among women aviators in 1929, when 99 women pilots joined together to offer mutual support and camaraderie to all women who were and who would become licensed pilots. The Ninety-Nines was born. This organization is now international in scope and welcomes interested women pilots, many of whom are members of ISA +21.

It is obvious the esteem in which Emily Warner is held by her sister members of ISA +21. She is seated in the center front during the 1998 celebration of ISA's 20th Anniversary. *Photo courtesy of ISA +21.*

Lori Cline explained, "ISA's emergence into the world of professional organizations was deliberately slow. It took time to become accepted as a group of knowledgeable women who would willingly share their experiences with others as well as provide assistance and encouragement for establishing a career in aviation. In the business world, networking by women's groups was just beginning to take hold and many of the members weren't sure they wanted ISA to venture beyond the bounds of socializing."

As the organization grew, so, too, did the need for more managerial leadership. The four roles of president, vice president, secretary, and treasurer had to expand to include an executive council with a nine-member board and the naming of several committees. At present, ISA welcomes all women pilots who are employed as flight crew members (Captain, First Officer, or Second Officer) and hold seniority numbers with an air carrier that operates under U.S. FAR Part 121, Part 129, or other international equivalent and which operates at least one aircraft with a gross weight of 90,000 pounds or more. Applicants need not be flying that aircraft themselves.

At a nominal rate, crewmembers and/or those interested in woman airline pilot issues can become members of ISA +21. A membership directory, roster, and an Airline Human Resources policy database are included with membership, as are numerous member outreach programs and scholarship distribution data. As begun in Nevada in 1978, the annual convention enhances membership and offers an opportunity for networking and mutual support. Offering outreach, ISA raises money for scholarships that help additional women follow their own careers in aviation; maintains a list of women aviators who are willing to speak at schools, scout troop meetings, clubs, and youth organizations; and provides a list of books, manuals, and videotapes that are available to members to help them reach their educational goals.

In addition, ISA has a Museum Committee that creates and maintains exhibitions that depict the stories of women's achievements in commercial aviation and seek to educate the public about women's contributions and capabilities. An AeroMedical committee supports its members with advice for the special medical considerations of female pilots and a Loss of License Committee is comprised of ISA members who have lost their flight status due to epilepsy or diabetes. For ISA members, a list of those members who have endured a particular medical procedure and who are willing to offer moral support to others facing the same medical processes is also maintained in a database. ISA's database on airline policies provides a source of information for pilots who wish to improve their own airline's policy or its union contact and its database for pioneering commercial pilots maintains a list of worldwide "Firsts" that are accessible to the public. This is just one location on the Internet in which Emily Howell Warner is named rightfully as the First U.S. woman to be hired as an airline pilot in the modern, jet-equipped scheduled airlines.

Lady Pilot
Just One of
the Boys Now

BY MARLENE CIMONS
Times Staff Writer

Headlines from the Los Angeles, California, Times, 16 January 1975

Author and Curator of Science and Technology for the MIT Museum, Boston, Massachusetts, Deborah Douglas wrote, in her Smithsonian Institution Press publication, "...United States airlines had experienced a long hiatus between the first woman commercial airline pilot (Helen Richey in the mid-1930s) and the next in the 1970s."

In a personal letter, Deborah continued, "The reason we treat Richey as a 'footnote' rather than a 'first' has to do with the fact that her career was short-lived, that despite her job title she was actually hired for another purpose— public relations. By contrast, the hiring of Emily Warner was not primarily public relations (although the airline certainly was happy for the recognition), but to work as a pilot. She flew and worked according to the same schedule as the male pilots and did so for an extended period of time.

"…What is important is the fact that society had changed its attitudes such that most of the airlines felt they could and should hire women. The Civil Rights Act of 1964 had precipitated a number of lawsuits which, in turn, made most corporations realize that they could not arbitrarily discriminate against women. Thus, by the early 1970s, the flood gates open—women get hired to be airline pilots, the military starts training women pilots, engineering and trade schools go co-ed, women get hired in management jobs at aerospace companies, and so forth. …Emily Warner symbolizes this new era."

ALPA, the Union of Air Line Pilots

As early as the 1920s, airline pilots recognized the value of an organization that would connect members of disparate airlines, would oversee aviation safety, crewmember and management disputes, labor contracts, and policies—in short, a labor union. To understand Emily's place as the first woman to be accepted as a member of ALPA, it is essential to know some of the history that went into the organizing of pilots into a union, some of the fighters who risked their careers for pilots' concerns, and some of the employee/management concerns that led to an early affiliation with the American Federation of Labor (AFL) and the growth of the Air Line Pilot Association—ALPA.

Having played a major role in elevating the career of the airline pilot to its respected and lucrative position, the organization occasionally has to remind even airline pilots of the difficulties their predecessors faced, the obstacles that they had to overcome. As George E. Hopkins wrote in Flying The Line, "Airline pilots should be well paid solely for the skills they possess and the responsibilities they bear, and in the ideal world they would be. But in the real world people get paid what they are worth only if they have the muscle to command it."

In the late 1920s, most airline owners were businessmen who were concerned with the commercial possibilities of catching a bit of the sky that Charles Lindbergh catapulted into prominence with his solo crossing of the Atlantic Ocean in 1927. Many were not only unable to fly, they were cavalier in their concept of aviators and confident that anyone could pilot an airplane.

Hopkins wrote, "Harris M. 'Pop' Hanshue, the operator of Western Air Express, …hated airplanes and never flew, even as a passenger, unless he had no other choice. W. A. 'Pat' Patterson of United was a banker who never so much as touched the controls of an airplane. Delta's C. E. Woolman …was essentially a promoter who stumbled into airline operations via his accidental control of a crop-dusting outfit. … Juan Trippe of Pan American flew the same way the notorious E. L. Cord of Century Air Lines flew—only when the weather was perfect and only with an experienced professional pilot along. Cord had a pivotal role in the pilots' growing support for ALPA because nobody better exemplified the contempt for pilots that most operators hardly bothered to conceal."

Although Errett Lobban Cord started his airline after the initial meeting of six pilots from three different airlines and was not directly responsible for the forming of ALPA, he nonetheless represented the managerial position that drove pilots to seek mutual support and to reach out to the American Federation of Labor (AFL) for additional clout. Two meetings—the first in Chicago in 1930 and the second, also in Chicago, in 1931—were instigated by a hard-driving David Behncke of Boeing Air Transport and, later, the first pilot listed for the airline that would become Northwest. Behncke spurred other pilots to recognize that airline operators were reducing their pilots' pay and that only in unity could pilots command proper remuneration. Within a year, he counted nearly half of the nation's pilots as members of his union and had completed affiliation with the AFL.

It was in direct opposition to an operator like E. L. Cord that ALPA was spawned. Cord was a ruthless entrepreneur who practiced cost effectiveness even to assessing the weight of paint to select the color [black] that weighed the least and therefore reduced the total weight of his painted airliners. Cord rose to preeminence and wealth through his interests in the Auburn automobile and in Checker cabs. He started Century Air Lines, which flew between Chicago, St. Louis, Cleveland, and Toledo, in 1931. This expanded into regional lines that operated in sections of the country and were appropriately named, as Century Pacific Airlines. Cord's airlines operated outside of the parameters set up by the Postal Service, which was paying for the delivery of air mail, by initially bypassing a request to carry mail. Pilots flying the mail were paid in the realm of $7,000 to as much as $12,000 per year. The stingy E. L. Cord found many pilots who were unemployed due to the Great Depression; he hired them for a mere $350 per month or $4,200 per year, with an additional $3 per hour for daytime and $5 per hour for nighttime flying. His goal was to eventually be a low bidder for the lucrative air mail contracts and reap the profits.

His other industries were known to offer low wages and to oppose unionization and his airlines were equally unfriendly to his employees. Century Pacific pilots had signed on with Dave Behncke and, when Cord tried to reduce their pay to a mere $150 per month, they called upon support from Behncke and ALPA. The pilots told Behncke that Cord had agreed to a 10-day hiatus prior to starting the lower salaries. At the end of the ten days, each reporting pilot was greeted by one of Cord's armed guards and escorted to a company employee who brandished a resignation paper and an application for employ at the $150 per month rate.

The pilots struck. Behncke attempted to negotiate, but his approaches were stymied by Cord, who had no intentions of losing. The ensuing fight brought in the Illinois State Federation of Labor and Behncke assessed each member of ALPA $25 to support the Century Pacific pilots during the battle.

Cord hired scabs to fly his line and, when Behncke attempted to meet each of them personally, Cord forced his new hires to, according to Hopkins, "live in a guarded dormitory, to take their meals together, and ride to and from the field on a bus with an armed guard. He also stationed armed guards to keep the strikers off the airfield."

Behncke properly claimed the airfield as public property and brought the Chicago City Council into the fray. Chicago's battle found its way to the floor of the House of Representatives in Washington, DC where Fiorello LaGuardia, a friend of Behncke's, railed against Cord. Unwisely, Cord persuaded an Indiana Congressman, Representative William Wood, to attack the very youthful ALPA, accusing it of being tied to racketeers of Chicago and of being communistic. LaGuardia was enraged that the pilots were so maligned; most of them had been trained by the U.S. military and still held reserve status. In part, LaGuardia countered that Cord's current pilots were lacking in qualifications, that his mechanics were poorly paid, and that his airplanes were unsafe.

ALPA proved itself a powerful force with which to deal. Cord sold Century Air Lines to American Airways in 1932; although, he didn't go away empty-handed. In selling his equipment, he realized 140,000 shares of stock in Aviation Corporation (AVCO, the parent company of American Airlines) and a controlling interest in American. He placed C. R. Smith in operational control while exercising his influence out of the public eye. The merger failed to help the striking Century Pacific pilots, but gave ALPA a reputation that attracted those pilots who had been hesitant about joining the union.

ALPA continues to provide representation for its members, including lobbying Congress and government agencies. It directs more than 20 percent of its income from dues to support aviation safety. Currently, under ALPA more than 600 working airline pilots, with a staff of professional aeronautical engineers and safety experts, serve on state and national committees that focus on safety. In most major airline accidents, ALPA representatives are usually granted "interested party" status, uniting ALPA accident investigators with the staff of the National Transportation Safety Board (NTSB). ALPA has played a role in either initiating or participating in many of the safety improvements in U.S. air transportation.

ALPA, which currently represents more than 53,000 airline pilots of the United States and Canada, is divided into groups that are reflective of particular airlines and are located in the airline's major hubs. Pilot Groups, each of which is governed by its elected Master Executive Council, focus on their internal affairs. Major policies are established by Local Council Representatives who comprise the Board of Directors. At the national level, an Executive Board and Executive Council provide guidance between biennial meetings of the Board of Directors. Four National Officers—the President, Vice President, Vice President of Administration, and Vice President of Finance—administer these policies from ALPA's offices in Washington, DC and Herndon, Virginia.

Its stated mission is: "to promote and champion all aspects of aviation safety throughout all segments of the aviation community; to represent, in both specific and general respects, the collective interests of all pilots in commercial aviation; to assist in collective bargaining activities on behalf of all pilots represented by the Association; to promote the health and welfare of the members of the Association before all governmental agencies; to be a strong, forceful advocate of the airline piloting profession, through all forms of media, and with the public at large; and to be the ultimate guardian and defender of the rights and privileges of the professional pilots who are members of the Association."

The first woman pilot to become an airline pilot in the modern jet-equipped fleet, the first to become a member of the previously all-male union, ALPA, and the first to become an airline Captain. *Photo courtesy of the Smithsonian's National Air & Space Museum Research Archives.*

The First Lady of ALPA

"When Frontier hired me," Emily said, "I was told about ALPA and was given a pep talk about the value of becoming a member. I was also told that all new hires serve a year of probation before even attempting to be accepted into ALPA. I was definitely interested. I believed that all I had to do was to successfully complete my first year on the line."

Honored as the Amelia Earhart Woman of the Year, Emily received a plaque
from Joe C. Moffitt of the Colorado Air National Guard, 1983.

Emily was not the only one entering an apprenticeship with Frontier and
ALPA. Joining her were David Sanctuary, John Andrews, Dan Cady, John
Bata, and Robert Ashby, the first black pilot hired by Frontier. Each received a
letter dated 8 May 1973 from John P. Giberson, then-ALPA Secretary. In part
Emily's letter stated, "We are pleased to advise you of your acceptance to
apprentice membership in the Air Line Pilots Association and enclose your
membership and lapel emblem. We have assigned you membership number
44715, FAL number 77 [Local Executive Council (LEC), Frontier Airlines
Number 77]. …We feel that in your joining with us we have gained a staunch
and loyal assistant in supporting the programs that will mean so much to the
personnel involved in aviation. When you are transferred from apprentice to
active membership an initiation fee will be owed based on your status at that
time— $25 for first and second officers, $50 for captains. As long as you are
on probationary status with the company, you will not be required to assume

any financial obligations. You will be notified of your transfer to active membership at the time the local council votes you to full membership."

Had Helen Richey lived to see the day, she would have been proud that a woman was finally anticipating the chance to become a bona fide member of the union that had turned her down. Along with her good wishes for Emily, she justifiably could have felt renewed distress over the treatment that she had received.

In December 1934, when Helen was hired by James D. Condon's Central Airlines to fly as a co-pilot, she was assigned to fly between Washington, Detroit, Cleveland, and Pittsburgh in the right seat of a Ford Trimotor. Without the restrictions of having to endure a probationary year, Helen applied promptly for membership in the Air Line Pilot Association (ALPA). It was not only denied, but the members of the all-male union sent a protest letter on 22

January 1935 to the Department of Commerce. The protest had nothing to do with her application for union membership; it had everything to do with her joining the airline as a co-pilot.

ALPA members suggested that the idea of a woman airline pilot was preposterous—as preposterous as seeing women operating locomotives or serving as ship captains. They brought up the subject of strength, insisting that a woman wouldn't have the strength necessary to control a large aircraft in blustery weather. They also asked where men would be if women were hired to pilot airliners.

The Department of Commerce told members of the union that Helen's service was already being tapered off—and this within one month of her hire. When it was noted that Helen was, although sporadically, still flying; the Department of Commerce contacted James Condon, who was finding it difficult to let her go. Her hiring had engendered a good deal of interest and several articles had been published in the nation's periodicals. Amelia Earhart, Helen's good friend and the one for whom she co-piloted in the Bendix Trophy Race of 1936, was then president of The Ninety-Nines. Happy for Helen, Amelia had announced the start of a new era that recognized the competence of women pilots. When Helen was denied admission to ALPA and denied her rightful place in the cockpit, she painfully realized that the job for which she had thought she was hired was not what she wanted at all. Saving Condon the trouble of phasing her out, she submitted her resignation.

According to Glenn Kerfoot in *Propeller Annie*, Amelia Earhart wrote, "One girl did succeed in landing a job recently as a copilot on one of the mail lines. What happened? Well, the pilot's union refused to take her in, not because of lack of ability—all of her co-workers admitted she was okay as to flying—but because she was a female. The result of this action was that the Department of Commerce refused to let her fly passengers in bad weather, so the poor girl could not do her part at all and had to resign."

Emily picked up the cudgel that Helen had carried. She met the scrutiny of members of ALPA and winds of change, chance, and opportunity were blowing in Emily's favor. Not only was she competent, but she had proven for a year that she fit into the cockpit as a crewmember who flew well, who conducted herself well, and who loved her job and gave it her all.

One male pilot in Frontier's Local Council #77, Jim Langhofer, blackballed Emily's application for ALPA. Before she was even hired, he'd gotten wind that Frontier was considering hiring her. Emily said, "He went into the front office and raised hell. He told them, 'You can't hire a woman!'"

"I flew with him as a second officer and he treated me okay; but, then, there was a co-pilot aboard, too. That served to temper the situation in the cockpit."

Despite his vigorous attempt to keep Emily out, Langhofer's negative vote was overruled. She said, with a smile, "A couple of years later, when I'd become pretty well accepted, one of the guys said to me, 'You know? We played golf with Jim the other day. Do you know what we have discovered? If we mention your name just as he's about to address the ball, it really ruins his game. It's a great way to win at golf."

Emily smiled. "I figured that was sweet justice."

Emily, second from right in back row, was invited to Washington, DC with other airline and military pilots in 1983 to participate in a panel discussion at the Smithsonian's National Air & Space Museum.

Emily missed the 1991 convention of ISA +21. These attendees, representing those who were encouraged by mentors like Emily, join the more than 12,000 women pilots who enjoy careers in today's U.S. airlines. They are appreciative of their Charter Members who organized them, inspired them, and who offered the networking possibilities that organization can bring. *Photo courtesy of ISA +21.*

CHAPTER 9: DEREGULATION AND UPHEAVAL

Student pilots are not required to demonstrate their ability to spin an aircraft, that is, to stall and autorotate around the longitudinal axis into what appears to be an almost vertical dive. The important aspect of the spinning aircraft, though, is that it is stalled. The wings are not equally creating lift and the recovery from a spin has to include a sharp forward pressure on the control yoke or stick to end the stall and obtain control over flight. Proper recovery requires sufficient altitude. In a metaphor for life, a spin can and does throw any well-ordered life into havoc. A spin can seem beyond control, but pilots are taught how to recover. Pilots are shown that few upsets to equilibrium are totally hopeless. So, too, in life.

As Emily upgraded to Captain in the Boeing 737 and faced the upheaval of airline deregulation, she simultaneously lived her private life on two fronts – in an apartment in the city of Denver and in a home that she and Jay built in Granby, high in the mountains to the west of Denver. One was as hurried and harried as the other was pastoral and tranquil. Denver represented the core for her career and for the schooling of her son, Stanley. Granby, where Jay thrived on designing and building beautiful high-beamed Timberpeg homes, meant an entirely different existence. There the architectural beauty of glowing wooden walls reflected the warm indoor lights and buffered the snow for which Colorado's winter high country is famous. Granby's scenic beauty represented leisure moments spent horseback riding, fishing, hiking, gardening, and, in the winter, sledding and cross-country and downhill skiing.

No parent escapes the challenge of having to inspire and motivate children – to develop their own interests, to appreciate the challenge of good educations, and to aspire to useful careers for their own futures. Parenting isn't an easy job. Stanley worried Emily. She, her ex-husband Stan, and Julius all gave of themselves to Stanley. They followed the doctor's advice and put him on Ritalin to help him stay in control of himself during his school days. "However," Emily said, "once he got into puberty, Ritalin didn't seem to work. His whole system was changing and adjustments were a struggle."

Emily moved their homes four different times in order to make sure that Stanley's schooling was the positive experience that was best for him. She interviewed different schools and tried to choose those with smaller classes and more favorable teacher-to-pupil ratios that would contribute to Stanley's education and his well-being. She, Jay, and Stan all helped him when they could. Like many young and hyperactive boys, Stanley vacillated; sometimes enjoying school and getting along with his superiors and with his fellow students and sometimes having difficulties.

"Stanley repeated the 9th Grade and that was good for him," she said. "He first attended his freshman year in a Jesuit School, and then he reentered his freshman year in a public school, Thomas Jefferson High School. That put him closer to his age group and brought Stanley into contact with an excellent school counselor who took him under her wing, encouraging him to go on to college. At home, Stanley loved to cook. He made complete dinners himself or he got a kick out of doing part of a dinner to help his Grandma or me."

Stanley went to Hastings College, a liberal arts college in Hasting, Nebraska, finding an aptitude for and an interest in drama. He started to work in film production companies and, when his friends left for California after graduation, he went with them and landed a job in film projection. After having been west for eight years, he began to sink into trouble with illegal drugs. It hasn't been established that there is a correlation between those who use substances like Ritalin as children to alleviate symptoms of hyperactivity or attention deficit disorders and those who abuse drugs as adults, but the possibility exists. At the very least, substance abuse, like an improperly recovered spin, can have tragic consequences. Emily had a deep love for her son and anguished over some of his choices. Her distress and her sense of helplessness were acute. She turned to the solace that she gained in flying, the comfort that being airborne could bring.

Airline Deregulation

Just as there was distress in her personal life, Emily faced distress and disruption in her career. Emily had survived two engine failures. The first was rather benign, an occurrence for which she had been trained and to which she responded quickly and almost instinctively. A minor mishap, it was simply the failure of one cylinder. The second occurred when she was a co-pilot with Frontier and flying with Captain Don Welch in a Boeing 737-200. "We took off from Kansas City," she told, "and we were about 88 miles to the west, climbing through 22,000 feet when, 'Boom!' Engine parts tore through, destroying the engine as they exploded. It was an immediate seizure. I was flying at the time and Don told me, 'Let's just start a gradual left turn and we'll return to Kansas City. I was always a pretty good stick and rudder pilot, so I must have immediately applied the right amount of rudder to counteract any yawing tendencies. Don radioed, telling Kansas City that we were returning and asking them 'to have equipment standing by, priority handling, please.'

"Don told me that he was going to radio maintenance, but that he was going to ask them not to contact us. He said, 'The trouble with maintenance is that they'll want to know every single thing that is going on every minute and they'll contact us when we're too busy to answer them.' What surprised me was that, within two minutes of the engine failure, there was a bang, bang, bang on the cockpit door. Three flight attendants had rushed to the cockpit, calling, 'What happened? What happened?' Nowadays, flight attendants would calm the passengers by telling them that something minor had occurred and that the crew was managing it. They wouldn't go up and bother the captain and first officer whose hands and heads are already busily engaged. Captain Welch was cool. He simply said, 'We've lost an engine. You go back and sit down and we'll get on the public address system and make an announcement to the passengers.

"Everything went like clockwork. We landed, no incident. We were fortunate that the weather was clear."

But the weather clouded precipitously when Deregulation hit the U.S. Airlines. The Civil Aeronautics Board (CAB) served from 1938 for forty years through the dramatic growth of United States' airlines. It accepted as its mandate the regulation of the industry. On 15 October, Congress approved the Airline Deregulation Act of 1978. The question of whether the airlines were strictly businesses or whether they were a public service proved a focal point for those for and those anti-deregulation. The question, to date, remains unanswered. Although the angst wasn't as personally devastating as her worry over her son, Emily's career was thrown into chaos.

"I thought I was going to retire from Frontier Airlines," Emily admitted. "The airline was doing just fine initially; but with deregulation, all kinds of upstart airlines came into being. Fare wars tore at the fabric of the U.S. airlines; small airlines were gobbled up by larger ones. It turned into a free-for-all. Most—though not all—of the big airlines weathered the storm, but smaller airlines were hit hard. Frontier started to get into trouble in 1983 and it was forced to close its doors in 1986.

"At that time, United was talking to us. We felt that it was a strong possibility that United would take us over and we even had a big sign hanging on our hangar that read, 'Thank You, United Air Lines.' But, management and the union got into a 'ballywag' about us. UAL wanted to hire our Frontier pilots at a lower pay grade than UAL pilots were receiving. ALPA wanted nothing to do with split pay grades. ALPA felt that, with intermixed and differing pay scales, it would weaken their position in future management contract disputes.

127

"Actually, later on they did initiate different pay scales. New hires, for example, are paid at a lower pay scale and it takes three years to make the greater amount. At the time, however, it was a blocking point. UAL planned to buy some airplanes from Frontier, but were not going to absorb the pilots. Then we were foundering.

"I was airborne one day and the tower operator called my aircraft, saying, 'Hey, Frontier. Did you hear the news? People Express just bought you.' In the cockpit, we groaned, 'Oh, no.'"

T.A. Heppenheimer wrote, in Turbulent Skies, "The founder of People Express, Donald Burr, had introduced cut-rate 'Peanuts' fares at his Texas International Airlines. ...In October 1985, he made his mistake. Hoping to maintain rapid growth, he purchased Frontier Airlines. It gave him a major hub in Denver and an expanded structure of routes and equipment and for one brief shining moment the acquisition made People the fifth-largest carrier in the nation. But Frontier was a traditional airline, complete with unions, bureaucracy, and free meals, and baggage service. Burr proceeded to turn it into his type of no-frills carrier—and quickly alienated Frontier's existing base of customers. Rival airlines responded with their own cut-rate fares and soon Frontier was on the ropes."

Emily knew that People Express was an upstart and that, in the melee that was deregulation, it was dedicated to provide passenger service at rock bottom fares and to operate without union members. Although she didn't know it at the time, People Express was doomed to close its doors as well. Before its demise, however, it managed to wreak havoc with Frontier, keeping it for only three or four months and bleeding off as many of its assets as possible. It was Burr who slammed the sinking Frontier into bankruptcy in August 1986.

Continental Air Lines stepped in, purchasing the remains of Frontier, including the pilot group. Emily explained, "We came in at a first officer pay, the same pay as other Continental first officers. But, the seniority list was convoluted and difficult. We all felt as if we had gotten the boot as far as seniority was concerned. Those Captains with Frontier who managed to remain as Captains with Continental ended up having to commute to places like Newark, New Jersey in order to hold the Captain's bid. Commuting is very hard on a person. To have to commute to go to work and to commute to have to return from work gets very tiring, especially if it is 2,000 miles from your home to your hub. It generally adds at least another day on either end of each trip.

"However, I flew for Continental for a month and a year. Although Frontier provided us with uniforms, we had to buy our own at Continental. Karen Kahn and Claudia Jones were already flying for Continental, so they and the other eight or ten women flying with Continental had figured out the 'problem' of a uniform for women pilots. Actually, it was Claudia Jones, who is now with Southwest Airlines, who designed a vee-necked, collarless suit jacket that is very sophisticated and very pretty. The uniform, completed with a white blouse with the option of a white tie that matched the blouse, was designed for a woman. It was in contrast to what I had worn—a man's suit jacket re-shaped."

Frontier's and Continental's Al Feldman

Of much greater upheaval than simply the commute, the captaincy, or the uniform, it was tragic to watch the demise of the man who had hired Emily and given her a place in aviation history. Al Feldman, having moved to Continental Air Lines, faced the battle of his life in trying to fight a takeover of his airline by Francisco Lorenzo, whose protégé had been Donald Burr. When Burr launched People Express, Lorenzo attempted to purchase the control of National Airlines. In the wild chaos that was deregulation, he failed in his attempted takeover, but managed to squeeze millions of dollars in profits during the financial donnybrook. He set up Texas Air Corporation as a holding company and created New York Air, pulling the same type of anti-union activities that had so enraged pilots dealing with E. L. Cord. In February 1981, he set his sights on a hostile takeover of Continental. Al Feldman was whipped at every attempt to stem the crushing defeat. In the midst of the 3 August 1981 strike of 13,000 air traffic controllers, facing sustained losses in his carrier and the personal tragedy of having lost his wife, Rose Emily, who had figured so importantly in Emily's hire, a depressed and a distressed Al Feldman took his own life.

Emily flew for Continental throughout 1987, grateful to have a job, and grateful to be piloting the Boeing 737-200, the airplane with the "old round dials." She adapted, despite her "demotion" from captain to first officer.

Her mother had recently needed to be put into her own quarters in St. Elizabeth's Nursing Home and Emily and Julius had moved into her mother's home to be closer to St. Elizabeth's and to clean, paint, and repair the house prior to putting it up for sale. Although Emily had been on stand-by, when told that her afternoon flight was cancelled, she went outside to shovel snow off the walk, thinking that she was no longer on reserve. She missed hearing the phone call that would have alerted her to fly. She went over to visit and have lunch with her mother and, when she returned home at around 3 in the afternoon, Continental's Flight 1713 had just crashed at Denver's airport. The aircraft took off with a captain and first officer aboard who were new to one another and new to the airplane. Perhaps there was sideload or some wake turbulence from a B-757 departing from a parallel runway. Flight 1713 rolled and struck the ground. Several people survived; but, several were killed. Emily recalled, "It was fate. I was not destined to be on that particular airplane and perhaps I was meant to be with my mother."

Included among those honored by Women In Aviation International as Pioneer Hall of Fame Inductees, Emily joins Eileen Collins, Fay Gillis Wells, Jeana Yeager, Peggy Baty Chabrian, and A. Mary Sterling. *Photo Courtesy of Parks College of St. Louis University.*

Deregulation Woes

"Deregulation," wrote Heppenheimer, "would offer no morality play that could contrast far-seeing wisdom of [Juan] Trippe with greedy folly of Lorenzo. As Eastern [Airlines] was spiraling to its end, Pan Am was meeting the same fate. Here the tale was both more poignant and more inexorable. Here was no corporate raider playing games with junk bonds, shuffling assets like cards in a poker hand, waging war against his own employees. Here was simply the slow but relentless decline of a major institution that could find no role in the era of deregulation."

For a pilot like Emily, flying for Continental worked out well for a while, despite the "games" that were being played in the corporate offices. "At first we Frontier pilots were still flying with our own, with the pilots we'd been accustomed to fly with," she explained. "But, the seniority lists were drastically changed. Frontier pilots went onto the lower rack, way at the bottom of all the captain's lists. I started being paired with young female Continental captains who were a lot younger than I. Here I am—the mother bunny—and I ended up being their co-pilot or first officer. That really bothered my vanity!"

She was well aware that, having been dropped even lower in a longer list of pilot officers, she would retire from flying at the mandatory age limit of 60 before she would ever get a chance to fly as a Captain again. "Once you've been in a Captain's position and you know you'll never get there again, that's distressing. I wanted to end my career in the left seat!"

One day during Emily's first month with Continental and having completed training, she was scheduled to fly as first officer with Captain Jack Gibson; she knew that the pairing would last for an entire month. "We got along all right," she said, "but I'd flown with him as a first officer at Frontier and knew that he was capable of giving people static. We got a push back from the gate and were getting ready to start the engines when I asked, 'Jack, would you stop the airplane for a minute?'

"He said, 'Sure,' wondering if something was wrong with the flight. He put on the brakes and looked around.

"I told him that nothing was wrong, I just wanted to get something straight with him. When he asked, 'What's that?' I said, "'I don't take bullshit anymore.'

"He just about fell out of his seat laughing. 'Emily! I can't believe you said that!' But, we went on to fly together all month and that month was a ball. He treated me fully as an equal and I took no more baloney whatsoever. It was really a lot of fun. I think he gained respect for me from that moment."

Exchanging Passengers for Cargo

In 1975, United Parcel Service (UPS), which had been founded on 28 August 1907, became the first package delivery company to serve every address in the continental United States and started operating in Canada. In addition to its vast fleet of trucks, UPS had started delivering cargo by airliners. These were leased aircraft until UPS announced plans to start an airline of its own.

Knowing that a start-up airline can hire pilots into positions, Emily applied to UPS; she had high hopes of being hired as a Captain.

When UPS started its messenger service in 1907, few U.S. homes boasted telephones and packages had to be delivered under private contract; the U.S. Postal Service (USPS) was still six years away from delivering parcels. A true entrepreneur, James Casey, then nineteen years old and living in Seattle, Washington, borrowed money and established the American Messenger Company. Casey demanded that his service provide low rates, twenty-four-hour delivery, reliability, and customer courtesy. His memory and his slogan, "Best Service and Lowest Rates," live on.

Garnering the market for delivering packages for retail stores, Casey, Evert McCabe, and Charles Soderstrom merged and became Merchants Parcel Delivery. They adopted the method of combining packages destined for a particular location into one delivery vehicle and saw their business grow and expand. Reaching as far south as Los Angeles, California, they opened United Air Express, but the air service fell victim to the bank failures of 1929 and ceased to operate after only eight months.

By the 1930s, packages were delivered across the west coast and branched out to include service in New York. George Smith joined the firm, which was now called United Parcel Service, and the familiar Pullman Brown color found its way onto all of the trucks and uniforms that represented UPS.

Winds of Chance

Shortages of raw materials like fuel and rubber caused UPS to make changes during the 1940s and 1950s. The company officials acquired "common carrier" rights to deliver packages between all addresses, private or commercial, and directly competed with the USPS. Initially, there were restrictions on operations in several parts of the nation. Federal Authority was necessary to cover interstate deliveries and State Authority was needed for intra-state deliveries. UPS sought authorization in the contiguous lower 48 states which was finally obtained by 1975.

Offering two-day service, UPS had reinstated its aerial delivery service in 1953, operating between major cities on the two coasts. To provide this service, the company used the cargo carrying capacity of the regularly scheduled airlines. By 1978, this delivery service was available in every state including Alaska and Hawaii.

Deregulation hit UPS just as hard as it hit pilots like Emily. Some routes were abandoned, some flights were reduced or cancelled, and some airlines, as we've seen with Frontier, were casualties of the deregulation. UPS opted to create its own jet cargo fleet and to make overnight delivery service a reality in the contiguous United States and Puerto Rico. Alaska and Hawaii were included later and international service was inaugurated. By 1988, when it was important to Emily that she be hired as a Captain and be given the chance to once again command an airliner, the FAA authorized UPS to operate its own airline.

"UPS had been contracting all of their pilots and airplanes through companies like Evergreen prior to the start-up of their own line," said Emily. "In the first phase of operation of an airline pilots can be hired directly into position. Captains were needed; first officers were needed. If a pilot had held that position in another airline, they could be interviewed and determined worthy of being hired directly into that role with UPS."

UPS Airline utilized a system of hubs that emanated like a spider's web from the home base in Louisville, Kentucky. Like a breath of fresh air after the shake-up that 1978 had brought, it was to this prestigious new airline that Emily pinned her hopes. She was in Chicago, Illinois, having flown a Continental B-737 into Midway Airport, when she was surprised by the motel telephone. The UPS chief pilot was calling to discuss her availability to start as a Boeing 727 Captain with their new line. Invited to jet to Louisville for an interview, she was offered first class flight arrangements and hotel accommodations. Emily, who admitted, "I almost fell off the bed!", was able to grab a Continental jumpseat and get to the February 1988 meeting. She accepted their offer.

Accustomed to having moved from house to apartment to condominium and back to houses in and around Denver, the timing was such that Emily and Julius were in the midst of another such move, this time as a result of having sold her mother's home. "We had gotten a contract on the house almost immediately. We found a condo at the Park Lane, I said to Julius, 'This one is your move,' and flew off to Louisville, Kentucky. I found a small buffet apartment close to the airport, started UPS flight training school in March, and spent the next six weeks transitioning into the Boeing 727. I did visit Julius when I could during the training and he came to see me in Louisville. We took advantage of the opportunity to see a couple of the Kentucky Derbies while I flew for UPS."

Emily donned the UPS Pullman brown uniform, filled a brown flight bag with her approach plates and en route charts, and carried her brown overcoat during the winter flights. Her transition was complete. It was 1988, she was a Captain and, as she climbed into the left seat for each flight, she enjoyed the feeling.

Winds of Change

Readying for takeoff one night, Emily's young female loader, obviously agitated, said, "I've got to close up the cargo compartment."

Emily saw packages still waiting to be put aboard and asked about them. The girl answered, "It's getting too close to schedule."

Emily could see fear in the girl's eyes and told her, "Listen, you go ahead and load the rest of those packages. I'll take the responsibility."

The girl, scared that someone would get after her for not having met her allotted time, hurried to complete her job. Emily noted, "It wasn't a problem. Once airborne, we made up the time and arrived on schedule."

Most of her UPS flights were of fairly short duration—one or two hour flights—with one or two stops per night. Most of the flying was accomplished between midnight and two in the morning and down time for loading and unloading could take up to three hours. Everything was based on hub system of gateway cities. Louisville was her domicile, but she often delivered to gateway cities like Pittsburgh, Pennsylvania; Salt Lake City, Utah; Ontario, California; Newark, New Jersey; or Chicago, Illinois.

Serendipity

In 1990, while Emily was on a UPS trip into Denver, she and her brother Dennis had gotten together to visit their mother in her nursing home. "I had finished my UPS training and was on a flying schedule. It was just happenstance that I had that particular flight into Denver on that particular night and that I had three or four hours the next day to be able to visit Mother. But, the Lord takes good care of everything. When Dennis and I were leaving, she waved to us from her wheelchair. She died that night.

"Early the next morning, I was due to fly off to Boise, Idaho, my next stop. I called UPS and they sent another Captain to relieve me. I could have been anywhere. Instead, there I was in Denver, just where I was supposed to be.

"My Dad always told me that true champions are not made by what they do in the normal realm of life. True champions are forged under pressure. Those words stayed with me. The times that I had to be the strongest were the times things were sliding downhill in a hurry—perhaps the weather was going to pot, you were on an instrument approach and you couldn't see ahead at all because of the blowing and swirling windswept snow, and you had to decide whether to press on with the landing or to abort and to divert. It was such times that my father's words came to me and strengthened my resolve. This was just as true in my private life as in my flying career.

"One night I was in Albuquerque and en route to Denver, only an hour's flight away. Our stop in Denver was always a short one, one that didn't allow me enough time to get home – just forty minutes or so. But, we were approaching Denver in miserable weather, although it hadn't dropped to the minimums, yet. I had a great co-pilot and a woman flight engineer with me and all three of us were working, constantly checking the weather, the ceilings, the visibility, and the temperatures and discussing our alternates. We'd chosen Cheyenne as our alternate and it wasn't boasting very good weather, either.

"It was late at night, which was par for the course with UPS; having known Denver all of my life, I was comfortable making an approach to 35 Right. But, the weather continued to worsen, the runways were getting covered with snow. We were second in line to land and the Continental pilot who landed ahead of us reported, 'Braking is nil.'

"In our Standard Operating Procedures (SOP) we were warned that when we heard a pilot state 'Braking is nil,' we were to abandon the approach. Inside of our cockpit, we looked at each other and I kept descending. I told my first officer, 'Ask that pilot to state the braking conditions again, please.'

"My co-pilot requested, 'Continental, are you sure that braking is nil?'

"This time the pilot understood what I wanted him to say and responded, 'Negative. Braking is fair to poor.' This gave us the legality to land and was recorded on the cockpit voice recorders. Just after we landed, however, Denver had to shut down its runways for a while. Our aircraft, the 727, had a good anti-skid braking system. I've been asked, 'Would I have made a different decision were I to have passengers in the back rather than packages of cargo?' My answer is, 'No. I was taking care of Number One. By taking good care of your own safety, you are effectively taking care of all who are under your command."

As Emily retired from UPS, Captain Terri Donner, who also flew for UPS, presented a bouquet and a clock as a retirement gift to Emily. Engraved on the clock was, "We're here because YOU were there."

In one of her more memorable flights, Emily was scheduled to fly from Newark, New Jersey to John F. Kennedy Airport in New York and to return. She said, "The weather was beautiful. I felt privileged to navigate around the brilliantly lit city – its lights reflecting in the waters of the Harbor, or swaying on the bridges or on some of the ships moving out to sea, or shining from the windows of the 'city that never sleeps.' It was a breathtaking sight and one of the reminders of the joys that are reserved almost solely for pilots."

On the other side of the continent, Emily piloted from Louisville to Anchorage, Alaska. She said, "One night I was assigned as a 'chase airplane.' That is, a fully loaded DC-8 was headed for Alaska. It was right before Thanksgiving and they couldn't get an additional 3,000 pounds of cargo onto the aircraft. UPS stipulates that it will deliver its packages on time, so they sent an additional B-727. The 3,000 pounds amounted to one container on my 727, which can accommodate eight large cargo containers or a total of 24,000 pounds.

"The carriage of one container didn't even pay for the flight, but, respectful of the Thanksgiving holiday and wanting to ensure that the cargo arrived on time, I was sent as chase plane after the DC-8. We went from Louisville to Boeing Field in Washington, refueled, and flew for five hours to Anchorage. The moon was so beautiful. It was one of the most beautiful scenes I've ever seen. The mountains were all white and the moon brightened the entire landscape as if it was the middle of the day. As we had to spend the night, the APU was kept running because of the intense cold. The baggage handlers wore special insulated suits so that they could work outdoors, but they are prevented from working more than 20 to 25 minutes outside in the frigid conditions.

"That night, I think it was about 30-below zero. We ferried the empty 727 back, again stopping to refuel at Boeing Field. It was the only Thanksgiving that I'd ever spent away from home and I was miserable about that; but, the flight had been fascinating."

Few consider the abrupt change of time zones that affect airline pilots. Emily found that her body didn't really like being a nocturnal animal and she found it rough to fly from the Eastern time zone to the Pacific time zone and to return in a matter of a few days.

Another flight took her from Louisville to JFK, no time zone changes; but, this time breaths came in slightly hushed intakes as she and her flight engineer noticed that the air stair warning light had come on. She said, "We talked it over and I decided that I'd like to descend. I knew I'd be happier at a lower altitude in case there was a reason to land quickly at an airport. We descended to 24,000 feet (Flight Level 240) and proceeded on toward JFK. Morning was just dawning and we could see the eerie bluish glow that spreads across the horizon just prior to the sun's breaking through. In the cockpit, those of us who flew at night pretended that the bluish glow was a signal that we had to get back into our coffins. Vampires have to sleep during the day!

"In the Boeing 727, the air stair is directly behind the fuselage at the tail of the aircraft. There is no way to get past all of the cargo to get back to visually check it. We knew that the light indicated that the stair wasn't completely hinged and closed, so I attempted to make one of the smoothest touchdowns possible.

"Controllers put us on a runway that gave us one turn into the UPS ramp. After touchdown, as we slowed, the air stair actually came down. The timing was fortunate. It would have been a greater hazard during the landing, extending down when the tail is low and the nosewheel not yet touching the runway.

"As it happened, we were on all of the wheels when a truck drove out signaling us to come to a full stop. We got out of the aircraft, leaving the repairs to the mechanics. I wrote the air stair up in the logbook and was surprised to get a call from the FAA at my hotel room that afternoon. I didn't think it was a big deal; but, of course, I was willing to answer questions. I'm sure there was enough airflow to hold it up while we were airborne, but as we landed and started to slow down, the air pressure eased the air stair extended slowly. There is a door at the top of those stairs, so there was never a threat to the containers filling the fuselage. The only damage was a minimal scraping to the base of the stair."

Winds of Opportunity

Emily flew with UPS from March 1988 to April of 1990, ironically becoming one of the Captains who held onto the bid by commuting almost 1,500 miles from home to fly her trips like those who'd moved from Frontier to Continental. The commute was taxing; the hours that she spent away were lonely. She admitted, "It was hard to sleep during the day and I developed terrible sleep patterns. Then, when I went home and tried to adjust – that was what got to me and, in the end, it was just too much. Flying for UPS was fascinating, but the schedule was difficult."

She began to reevaluate her goals.

"I flew into Denver at about 4:30 one morning in 1990 and saw an old friend from Frontier, Dale Buss. He wanted to board my aircraft to do a ramp check. I was surprised. 'A ramp check? What's this all about?'"

Dale had taken a job with the FAA. They had time to talk briefly.

Emily had applied to work for the FAA when Frontier closed its doors and she had gotten on the register, but the job offer that she received would have required a move to Syracuse, New York. "That wasn't where I wanted to be. Dale explained how he'd gotten his Denver FAA position and the idea simmered like a warm pot of soup on the back burner of the stove. What a break that would be to have an opening here in Denver for me."

Dale suggested that Emily apply once again. She admitted, "The more I thought about it, the better the idea sounded and the more intrigued I became. I was ready to make a move back to Denver, if it was remotely possible. I got an SF 171, a lengthy application for employment and an interview all in one."

Back in her apartment in Louisville, Kentucky, Emily attacked the governmental form, borrowed a typewriter, and proceeded to work on her résumé. How many times had she written an application and then updated the form? It seemed to have been an endless cycle of paperwork. This time she requested notification that her application had reached the FAA in Oklahoma City and she let Dale Buss know that she was seriously interested in any opening that might exist or come into being in the Denver FAA Office.

Within a few weeks, a response returned from Oklahoma City and an announcement was made of an opening in Denver. She was urged to apply for that specific position. The paperwork resumed. Within four months, she was invited to interview with Del Gregg and Frank Hollander in Denver.

"I was totally qualified – current and experienced. I didn't know who I might have been competing with, but I was sure that I was as well qualified as I could possibly be. I don't know of any of the other applicants, but I was gratified to get the job. It was July 1990 and I was raring to move back to Denver.

"Julius and I took a vacation. We drove to Monterrey, California to spend a weekend with Stanley and we took the time to be together for a while. I knew that working with the FAA would entail a training session in Oklahoma City at the FAA Academy. But, the time would be short and it was good to know that neither Ok City nor the Denver FAA office would be as far from home as Louisville, Kentucky."

**Emily and Jay Warner enjoy Emily's Golden Moment – her Induction into
the National Women's Hall of Fame, Seneca Falls, New York, 4 October 2002**

CHAPTER 10: THE FAA, BACK TO THE B-737

There is something very special about coming home. As much as Emily had loved flying with a profitable and growing cargo airline, she needed to be at home with Julius, to strengthen the love that they'd built during their 14 years of marriage, and to re-emphasize and cherish the bonds of their marriage. She and Julius had managed to see each other quite often while she was domiciled in Kentucky with UPS; but, she knew that they had both missed the sharing of living together. Their marriage was a good one; affection and closeness could make it even better.

Joining Emily and Jay as her permanent exhibit is unveiled in Denver's
Wings Over the Rockies Museum were six grateful and supportive women airline pilots.

Denver itself seemed to welcome her back. She loved the familiarity of her city and, having learned what was expected of her through her employment with the FAA, she eagerly anticipated contributing to the aviation in which she'd invested so much.

Her return to Denver was important to Stanley, too. Stanley was on his own; he had long since left the nest and settled in California where he moved in his own circles. Nearing the age of 30, however, Stanley's life reflected the turmoil that had characterized his coming of age.

Julius extended as much help as possible, but it was Emily and Stan Howell who truly anguished over their son Stanley's difficulties. Stan Howell had spent his career as a medical caregiver, first with elderly patients, then in emergency services at Denver General Hospital, and also in the Denver Care Center. At the latter, his patients were those trying to rid themselves of drug addictions. But, even those trained to recognize the symptoms and know of the pitfalls of any addiction are helpless in the face of loved ones who cannot seem to gain control over their own choices.

Emily and Stan had repeatedly seen that Stanley receive care. He had entered a month-long program in Castle Rock, a small Colorado town south of Denver. He'd taken a year-long program sponsored by the Salvation Army and Emily and Stan had visited him, in the programs and when he was moved to Safe House situations at the programs' ends. Stanley lived with his father for more than a year as well.

Stanley wasn't healthy; the friends with whom he surrounded himself weren't healthy or strong. His struggles were exacerbated when one of his closest cousins, Neil, died of a sudden heart attack at the age of 28. Neil's sister, Theresa, interceded. She brought Stanley home from California in an effort to help. Neil and Theresa's mother, Stanley's Aunt Jan, had died at the age of 48. These were depressing realities of life.

Always infatuated with drama and with theater arts, 35-year-old Stanley chose to return to California. There, too, he entered rehabilitation programs and moved eventually to another Safe House. But, in November 2001, Emily was notified that Stanley had died. A diabetic, he'd succumbed to heart failure. As if the tragedy wasn't painful enough, Emily returned from having made arrangements for his burial to find the first and last e-mail message that Stanley had sent to her. Dated the day before he died, he wrote, "Hi Mom! I finally figured out how to use this E-mail thing so here it is, my first E-mail. I'm looking forward to seeing you on 11/5 and I am still trying to figure out a place we could dine when you arrive. I'll try to drop a message on your e-mail now and again. Everything is the same as when I talked to you last and I am feeling very optimistic about my future if the course remains the same. Please send anyone else's e-mail address (Theresa's, Garrett Howell's, etc.) …I'll talk to you soon. Love, Stan."

A heartbroken mother had nothing further that she could do for her son. But, reaching out to help others, Emily contributed and continues to contribute by giving of herself through her church, through contributions to places like the Good Samaritan House, and by spending time at homeless shelters. She said, "It is sad to see ruin in the lives of professionals, of young people, and of others among the homeless. Drugs destroy families throughout all socio-economic levels, throughout the range of religious affiliations, and throughout educational and occupational realms.

"I used flying to help me get my own life back on track. Being able to fly has been a savior to me when I faced tough times. I guess it pinpoints the one reason that I love pilots. People who get involved in flying are different. They have goals and aspirations."

Joining the Federal Aviation Administration

In 1990, Emily left behind her Captain's status and returned to the jump seat in which she'd started in Boeing 737s. She became a part of the Federal Aviation Administration and was assigned to the United Air Lines Boeing 737-300/500 fleet as an Air Crew Program Manager. As with any new job, however, it started with the ten weeks of indoctrination required. Julius drove her to Oklahoma City for her courses of training and returned every other week so that they could spend time together. She said, "When I went with the FAA, I went through United's full Boeing 737-300 school as a captain with another first officer. It was transitional training. The 737-200 that I'd flown differed from the 737-300 in that the 300 has the 'glass' cockpit – everything is computerized: flight management systems, moving maps, and so forth. It's a slightly larger airplane and has bigger engines than the B-737-200. The twin-engine 737-500 is the smallest of this series of airplane, with seats for 110 passengers. The 737-300 seats 126 passengers. Both aircraft share the new high-tech flight deck, so pilots qualified in the 300 can also fly the 500."

But the B-737s waited in her future for a year. Initially Emily took a position in Denver's Flight Standards District Office (FSDO) as an Aviation Safety Inspector. Although she accepted several different tasks, one particular aircraft accident stood out in her mind. She said, "I investigated the crash of a Cessna 210 with an experienced Accident Investigator named Mr. Gonzalez. This single engine aircraft crashed in Buena Vista, two hours south of Denver. No one was killed, which was miraculous as the craft carried five passengers including a small baby and landed upside down on the airport, but off-runway. The pilot was flying the craft at night and he ran it out of fuel. That was the one good thing about the accident as, empty of fuel, he avoided the extra hazards of an explosion or a fire. Mr. Gonzalez and I spoke with the pilot and, as we walked away from the interview, he said, 'That guy is lying through his teeth.'"

In addition to the pilot, Emily interviewed the paramedics and the firemen who responded to the crash site as well as a representative of the company from which the pilot rented the airplane. The pilot, who had a Private license only, was guilty of several violations. He attempted to operate for hire and charged passengers $150 per person to fly them between Denver and Phoenix,

Arizona. He found passengers by blatantly advertising in the Rocky Mountain News. The investigator and Emily built the case slowly, obtaining copies of the newspaper ads in addition to gathering information in the interviews. The pilot was overloading the aircraft, he was flying above 10,000 feet with no oxygen for his passengers, and, most damning, his blood sample, taken at the time of the accident, revealed a recent use of marijuana. Once the file was completed, it went to FAA lawyers in Seattle and resulted in a revocation of the pilot's license.

From the FSDO, Emily moved to the FAA Certificate Management Field Office (FCMFO), which is the flight operations and training section of the main FCMFO that is based in San Francisco. As Air Crew Program Manager for the United Air Lines Boeing 737-300/500 Fleet, Emily's functions differed daily, but revolved around duties that tied her to the United Air Lines Training Center and to the aircrews undergoing a variety of training scenarios.

Part of the esoteric camaraderie of aviation is the language, verbiage known to aviators alone. In an alphabet soup of descriptors, Emily tossed out such terms as PC, AQP, LOFT, LOE, CQP, and CRM; or, Pilot Check, Advanced Qualification Program, Line-Oriented Flight Training, Line Operational Evaluation, Continuing Qualification Program, and Cockpit Resource Management.

The PC is the annual checkride that is administered to every airline pilot. PCs are conducted in simulators, currently greatly enhanced from the Convair 580 sim in which Emily was tested. At the United Air Lines Training Center, the simulators are full motion machines that are made by CAE, a Canadian firm that is a global enterprise.

United Air Lines' CAE Simulators are full motion machines, maintained in virtually sterile conditions and used extensively in the training and testing of airline pilots.

Emily submitted to an annual Pilot Check like every other airline pilot. Her last PC was with Check Pilot Bill Knell on 13 July 2000, CAE simulator, United Air Lines Training Center, Denver.

Emily described the AQP as "a living organism." She explained, "The training for the Advanced Qualification Program can be tailored to specific individuals and therefore can focus upon the needs of those persons and can change as requirements dictate. The AQP Certification Ride is a set of events, a scripted plan. The Standards Captain who administers the check ride has a set of triggers, which can be varied from something simple like a pressurization problem or a sick passenger in the cabin to a serious problem like a loss of hydraulics. Every challenge that the crewmembers face can be distracters from the jobs they are required to do. They have to be able to handle the distractions and get the airplane on the ground safely. The primary goal is overall effectiveness as a crew."

Accident investigations like the Cessna 210 crash in which she participated have indicated particular needs for a variety of training scenarios and those become the emergencies that are practiced.

She said, "Remember in pilot training in the past? We learned to introduce, recognize, and recover from unusual attitudes. Progressively, those have been taken out of pilot training and pilots are suffering the omissions. The steepest bank that became required was a 45-degree bank. Pilots never saw upside down; they never saw an unusual attitude. Event Oriented Training has evolved due to those omissions. Advance Maneuver Training is returning and, in modern simulators with full movement, the 'airplane' can be put into an inverted 135-degree angle to the ground—an inverted descent. The only way to recover is to put the aircraft in knife-edged flight, a 90-degree bank, come through the horizon and split-S to recover the use of the elevator control. Thanks to the advanced simulators, we can do rolls. Pilots need the training, as witnessed from some of the accidents that have occurred."

In Line Oriented Evaluations, Emily's job was judgmental. She watched the conduct of crewmembers as they worked in synchronization with one another. She analyzed how the Captain handled his or her relationship with the first officer; how crewmembers related to one another as they solved the tasks expected of them; and how those relationships changed in sudden emergency situations. She said, "I had to evaluate; I had to judge. One crew might have been outstanding; another might have performed to standard; but personally, I thought they failed to do as well as another crew. My job was to admit that I was looking at certain aspects and that the crew had to be rated as standard, above standard, or below. I had to look beyond personalities and be as objective as possible. It was very interesting. And, it was hard to be completely impartial. I had to ask, 'Is the crew working together? Are they using all the skills available to them?' It was a very interesting job."

Emily's daily tasks might have included actually flying in a B-737-300/500 aircraft administering an en route inspection or a certification check of one of the airline pilots in the cockpit, attending a weekly office meeting, or traveling for the various training programs required that keep air crew program managers up to date.

Evaluating whether a captain and his or her crewmembers worked harmoniously as they created new ways for differing personalities to become a cohesive and cooperative crew was Emily's forte. She had been required to become a cooperative crewmember from the first time that she boarded an airliner as a pilot. Not everyone is a born leader, but much of what the FAA is trying to accomplish is to bring out that quality and to have it work in conjunction with all of the resources at the leader's command. Emily had learned to accept the leadership of others and, in so doing, had honed her own leadership skills. Few knew as intimately as she the necessity for harmony to exist between the two or three persons in the cockpit and those who intercede between the cockpit and the passengers. Again, she was the right woman in the right place and at the right time.

United Air Lines, like Delta and some of the others, initiated a program that fell under the acronym CRM, Cockpit Resource Management, and referred to the proper management of all available resources when handling routine as well as unexpected cockpit duties. Captains accepted responsibility for the safe conduct of their flights and were the titular heads of the flights, but modern airlines expect, now, that the days of having the Captain exercise complete control irrespective of input from crewmembers are over. CRM is taught to emphasize the use of all resources that are available in any situation that is out of the ordinary. Flight Attendants, any airline personnel who might be traveling as passengers on the aircraft, mechanics who can be reached by radio, air traffic controllers—all can contribute to the safety of a flight whenever it was necessary and whenever they were called upon.

Emily had one go-around with a Captain when she was a first officer. A flirt, he had his eyes on one of the Flight Attendants. He turned to Emily, his assigned co-pilot, and asked, "Would you mind going to the back and letting that Flight Attendant come up here to the cockpit for a while?" Emily was flabbergasted. She was new; she was trying to find a place for herself in what had been a man's domain. She knew that the Captain's request was wrong; she also knew that it was her place to follow directions. Taken aback, she did as the Captain requested, took a seat in the passenger cabin, then simmered angrily that such an event had even occurred. It wasn't right. It should not have happened. Had there been an emergency, it would have been disastrous to have the second pilot no where near the controls. It infuriated her that he'd asked and it infuriated her that she'd acquiesced.

With CRM, that Captain could no longer even think of making such a request. The cockpit is an arena in which there is mutual concern and mutual responsibility. All members of the crew are essential to the safety of the flight and all members of the crew accept responsibility for the safety of the flight under the leadership and guidance of the captain.

Emily said, "I've heard speakers discuss the Zero Accident Factor, but that is impossible. The best that we can work toward is greater safety. We analyzed the last forty years of aviation and recognized that check rides hadn't kept up with changes in the industry and in the aircraft themselves. The crew philosophy never changed until the advent of CRM."

To enhance flight safety, airline personnel have devised training sessions that are aimed at addressing the communication and coordination necessary to ensure the safest possible flight. There have been two classic cases that illustrate CRM: one involving a Boeing 737 of Aloha Airlines and the other is the DC-10 that crash-landed at Sioux City, Iowa.

In the first, on 28 April 1988, Emily's friend, Mimi Tompkins, was then a First Officer aboard Aloha Airlines Flight 243. She was at the controls flying her leg, which was to fly from Hilo to Honolulu at 24,000 feet. Her Captain performed the non-flying duties for that portion of the flight. Upon leveling at altitude, a loud "whoosh' was heard as a huge portion of the jet's fuselage peeled away and the jet experienced rapid decompression. One flight attendant was dragged out of the aircraft to her death, a second flight attendant was thrown to the floor with severe lacerations, and the third, also thrown to the floor, managed to crawl the length of the exposed fuselage, tending to passengers. Using all of the resources available to them, the captain and Mimi Tompkins performed the remarkable service of nursing the stricken airplane to an emergency landing on Maui. As the captain took the controls, Mimi tuned the radio to the emergency frequency, declared an emergency, requested an alternate landing on Maui, and called for emergency assistance. There was no way to communicate with the flight attendants and Mimi had no way of knowing that her transmissions were being received. She and the captain used hand signals to communicate with one another and the two went to the extreme and called upon strengths neither had previously had to display. An incredible amount of damage occurred and, remarkably, the one flight crew member was the sole fatality. From a total of 89 passengers, five crew, and one air traffic controller who occupied the jump seat in the cabin, it was incredible that 29 escaped injury, 57 suffered minor injuries, eight persons were seriously injured, and the one crewmember was lost. One glance at a photograph of the aircraft emphasizes just how remarkably the crew performed.

Emily's friend Mimi Tompkins was First Officer aboard Aloha Airlines Flight 243 on 28 April 1988 when the fuselage tore from the airframe and forward passengers occupied a gaping hole. Miraculously, using all available resources, Mimi and the crew nursed the stricken airplane to a landing.

On 19 July 1989, Captain Al Haynes was called upon to exert a similarly Herculean effort. He piloted United Air Lines DC-10 Flight 232 out of Denver and, at 37,000 feet, the aircraft lost its number two engine. Haynes said, later, "The DC-10 has three completely independent hydraulic systems. When the number two engine blew, it took out the hydraulics for the number two section. Some 70 pieces of shrapnel penetrated the horizontal stabilizer severing the number one and number three lines. The net result? We ended up with no hydraulics. ...We had no ailerons to bank the airplane, no rudder to turn it, no elevators to control the pitch, no leading-edge flaps or slats to slow the airplane down, and no trailing-edge flaps for landing. We had no spoilers on the wing to help us get down or help us slow down once we were on the ground. On the ground, we had no steering and no brakes."

Emily said, "Al Haynes used every resource possible. He called on a flight training manager, an instructor in the Douglas DC-10, who happened to be in the passenger cabin to come forward to help with the throttles. He put someone in charge of every different phase of that airplane. They couldn't even duplicate what he did in a simulator because he got everybody working together in a unique way."

Having experienced the unbelievable failure of all hydraulics, it is miraculous – and a credit to Cockpit Resource Management – that 184 of the 296 persons aboard survived this 19 July 1989 crash of Captain Al Haynes' United Air Lines DC-10 Flight 232.

Haynes, an impressive speaker, is quoted as having said, "I am firmly convinced that the best preparation we had is a program that United Air Lines started in 1980 called Command Leadership Resource Management (CLRM) training. It is now referred to as Cockpit Resource Management (CRM).

"Up until 1980, we worked on the traditional concept that the captain is THE authority on the aircraft," wrote Al Haynes. "What he says goes and his decisions are not to be questioned. We lost a few airplanes because of that. Sometimes the captain isn't as smart as we like to think he is. [On 19 July 1989] we had 103 years of flying experience there in the cockpit, trying to get that airplane on the ground. Between us, we had not one minute of practicing or experiencing total hydraulic failure, so why would I know more about getting that airplane on the ground under those conditions than the other three? If I hadn't used CRM, if we had not let everybody contribute their knowledge and ideas, it's a cinch that we wouldn't have made it."

Captain Haynes named five factors for which he was grateful. Luck – the weather was clear, it was mid-afternoon, the aircraft was over the flatlands of Iowa, and it was shift-change at the medical facilities in Sioux City, Iowa, doubling the numbers of available medical personnel. Communication – second officer Dudley Dvorak alerted the Chicago Crisis Center and UAL's Chicago dispatch center. UAL personnel involved in aviation accidents arrived in Sioux City before Al Haynes was admitted to his room in the hospital. Controllers helped immeasurably and the senior flight attendant, upon receiving word of the emergency, carried out all of her duties and involved the rest of the flight attendants. Preparation – the trauma crews and emergency personnel in Sioux City had practiced a simulated emergency in 1987 and forewarning had brought 285 members of the National Guard to the field at the ready. Execution – calling upon each trained crewmember to give more than his or her share and having each do so. Finally, Cooperation – it was Children's Day on this UAL flight and attendants had adults move their seats so that no child was left without an adult, people asked to man the emergency exits did so ably and willingly, and persons on the ground saw to it that there were places for everyone to be sheltered and fed. There were 112 fatalities in the crash landing of Flight 232, but, miraculously, there were 184 who survived. Al Haynes continues to talk about CRM and its extraordinary value to every flight crew. His story has inspired Emily countless times since 1989 and served as an excellent example of all that she encouraged among the flight crews with whom she worked.

The Wings Over the Rockies Museum in Denver boasts a permanent exhibition devoted to Emily and focuses upon her illustrious career.

Emily hadn't ended her airline piloting career when she took her position with the FAA. Close ties held her to the airlines as she worked in the United Air Lines Training Facility, flew often with cockpit crewmembers in simulated and in actual flight, and performed at Government Service Level 14, an admirable career position surrounded by the airline crewmembers with whom she had much in common.

With more than 22,000 flying hours in her logbooks, Emily retired from the FAA in 2002, taking her final flight in an Airbus 300. This combined a check flight for the crew with a gala farewell party in New Orleans for the lady who really meant it when she said, "I'm from the FAA; I'm here to help you."

Emily was delighted to meet the daughter of Charles and Anne Morrow Lindbergh in Dayton, Ohio when Reeve Lindbergh Tripp was in town signing her book, *Nobody Owns the Sky*. Reeve's book tells the story of Bessie Coleman, the first U.S. black to obtain a pilot's certification. Later, Bessie Coleman and Emily, two of only nine of the century's women involved in aerospace, were inducted together into the National Women's Hall of Fame, Seneca Falls, New York.

CHAPTER 11: BUILDING THE BEACH

Emily Hanrahan Howell Warner shattered any limits that cocooned male pilots in the cockpits of scheduled U.S. airliners. A few women had gained access to airliner controls prior to Emily's hire, but none had kept men from having to share their illustrious careers with women pilots. Proving in 1973 that she was the right woman in the right place at the right time, Emily relied on her rare combination of character traits to enter and succeed in a previously all-male environment. Those traits have remained with her throughout her successful career. Where another might use bluster and belligerence, Emily has exuded patience and grace. Foregoing legal action or "in-your-face" demands for equal opportunity, Emily has demonstrated excellence. She earned respect in her command positions, practices fairness and competence in her dealings, and depended upon her iron will when the going got tough. She answered criticism with capability; she responded to negative comments with wit. The model of persistence, she uniquely blended her determination with poise. Someone once said of her, "If God had meant for a woman to fly, He would have made her like this woman."

Retirement never hung like a heavy and dreaded albatross on Emily's shoulders. Retirement represented a challenge, a new direction, and refreshing change, as it does for all vital and dynamic retirees. In retirement she could be free to do consulting work for the FAA; she could mentor young women, urging them to consider career fields in aviation. In retirement, capitalizing on a quote that she'd taken to heart, she could urge them to "build the beach."

She recalled having thought about and truly appreciating her good fortune as an eighteen-year-old, riding the bus from North Denver to take flying lessons. "How many girls get a chance to do this?" she thought at the time. In addition, the bus ride necessitated a trip through the center of the city and a transfer through an area known as "Five Points," and then it continued down 32nd Avenue to Stapleton Airport. That particular street is now called Martin Luther King Boulevard.

Emily said, "After I started flying, I bussed out there on my day off each week. I could only afford one flight lesson a week and it almost became a religion to me. I was extremely determined to save my money and make certain that I didn't miss out on that special weekly lesson. One time, when I was passing through Five Points, it came to me how lucky I really was. I was following though on a challenge to do something that most women don't do. I was aware, as I looked out of the window and saw that most of the people were black, that I was lucky that I wasn't black. I recognized that, as a young white girl, I had opportunities that were more available to me. I wondered just what opportunities were open to black girls. Of course, I didn't know about Bessie Coleman, or Janet Bragg, or Willa Brown, or Mildred Carter at that time. When I learned about them later in my life, I recognized that it had been a lot tougher for them to get their pilot licenses. I was glad that they, too, had persevered."

TERRORISM!

Devastatingly, 11 September 2001 shattered any rational aviator's image of invulnerability and control. The airliners that had once evinced images of the lofty and the adventurous, the free and the bold, explorers and travelers, were used as weapons of mass destruction. In a flaming hell loosed on our nation, our own airliners were wrenched from the control of American and United Air Lines' pilots. Distorted into missiles, instead of safe transportation and exciting flight, they exacted violent murder of the innocents from many nations who were in the aircraft or who were destroyed in the buildings and on the ground.

It is horrifying to read or witness a television news broadcast about 11 September 2001. It is another thing to have spent more than a decade involved with the training of United Air Lines crewmembers and to be able to recognize names and faces among the victims. The reality of the almost incomprehensible loss haunts those who knew them. Emily lost acquaintances on 11 September 2001 and she would never forget them.

Aboard United Air Lines Flight 93, the Boeing 757 that augured into the ground in Pennsylvania, were: Captain Jason Dahl, First Officer LeRoy Homer, and flight attendants: Lorraine Bay, Wanda Green, Cee Cee Lyles, and Sandra Bradshaw. Aboard United Air Lines Flight 175, which exploded in the World Trade Center, were: Captain Victor Saracini, First Officer Michael Horrocks, and Flight Attendants: Robert J. Fangman, Amy N. Jarret, Amy R. King, Kathryn L. Laborie, Alfred G. Marchand, Michael C. Tarrou, and Alicia N. Titus.

Emily didn't know the American Airlines crewmembers, but she felt heartsick that vile extremists would choose the airplanes that she'd loved so long to perpetrate their despicable deeds. None of her hours of training nor her 25,000 flying hours of experience prepared her to comprehend such morally depraved behavior. Aboard American Airlines Flight 11, which slammed into the World Trade Center, were: Captain John Ogonowski, First Officer Thomas McGuinness, and Flight Attendants: Barbara Jean Arestegui, Jeffrey Collman, Sara Low, Karen Martin, Kathleen Nicosia, Betty Ong, Jean Roger, Dianne Snyder, and Madeline Sweeney. Aboard American Airlines Flight 77, which struck the Pentagon, were: Captain Charles Burlingame; First Officer David Charlebois; and Flight Attendants: Michele Heidenberger, Jennifer Lewis and her husband, Kenneth Lewis, and Renee May. A retired American Airlines pilot and U.S. Navy Admiral, Wilson Flagg and his wife were passengers.

She could picture the face and the confident smile of the UAL Captain who undoubtedly signed his airplane's release without even a shadow of a doubt that he could pilot his flight to a safe landing. It wouldn't have crossed

161

his mind that he, the crew, and all of his passengers would die at the hands of warped individuals whose hatred consumed them and who were convinced that they would know rewards in another life. He would have resisted with every fiber of his being the idea that the airplane that he commanded would kill the persons who entrusted their lives to him.

Emily couldn't have known the horrifying last few moments of life for the captains, their crew, and their passengers; but, she could well imagine that it was spent in anguish and despair, ending swiftly in vicious, explosive annihilation. It was only later that she and the rest of the mourning nation could fathom that colossal fireballs in Pennsylvania, Virginia, and New York City were caused by those imbued with an extremist fundamentalism, their hatred fanned over years of indoctrination, their reasoning clouded with a determination to wreak havoc, death, and destruction upon the United States. Is that why they chose airlines named United and American? Was it simply convenient scheduling or did the very names rally those intent on bloodshed and terror?

For Emily, this entirely new, unpredictable, and frightening enemy required strong and decisive changes to take place in her aviation world. The training manuals that once had exhorted crewmembers faced with hijackers to be docile and calmly persuasive proved to be woefully inadequate. The Federal Aviation Administration and all of the nation's airlines suddenly had to begin training their crewmembers to face an enemy who was willing to die and who wanted to take thousands of innocent lives. In retirement, Emily's experience and expertise as an airline pilot and as an Air Crew Manager would be valuable in a consulting position.

Anticipating working part time, she arranged her schedules appropriately. She hoped to set aside the time, still grieving over the loss of her son, to give of herself to Catholic Charities, to visit the homeless and the aged as she had volunteered at the Mullen Home for the Sick Poor during high school. She eagerly looked forward to mentoring young people and encouraging them toward lofty goals of careers in aviation and aerospace. She threw her prodigious energies toward the programs and exhibits of Wings Over the Rockies Air and Space Museum and its hands-on outreach program designed for educating Denver's school children.

Having consistently proven her capability, she contributed to furthering women's opportunities. Emily said, "Although gender is no longer an issue in the airline employment office, a woman won't get the job simply by default— just because she is a woman. She will have to have the right stuff in the cockpit. What exists today and existed yesterday is the necessity to prove that you can handle the yoke—that you can fly safely and well. Flying is so intense and such a professional career, what matters is capability. There is no place for the gender issue anymore."

Emily and Jay Warner savor the special moment, Emily's demonstration of having met the qualifications of the stated mission of the National Women's Hall of Fame: "To honor in perpetuity those women, citizens of the United States of America, whose contributions to the arts, athletics, business, education, government, the humanities, philanthropy, and science have been the greatest value for the development of their country." Emily was proud to "Stand Among Great Women."

A Singular Honor

In October 2001, a scant month after the tragedy of 11 September, Emily had been planning on induction into the prestigious National Women's Hall of Fame in Seneca Falls, New York. In the aftermath of the attack on our nation, the induction was cancelled. A year later, invited to "Stand with Great Women," all 2001 and 2002 Inductees were honored in one exceptionally elegant ceremony during the weekend of 3-5 October 2002. Implicit in being installed in the National Women's Hall of Fame and joining the ranks of such notables as Willa Cather, Mary Cassatt, and Margaret Bourke White was the recognition that Emily, like the other Great Women, made enduring contributions to the development of our nation and could be counted among the exceptional American women of the century.

Emily was seated with her niece, Theresa, and her husband, Jay, prior to the induction into the prestigious National Women's Hall of Fame, Seneca Falls, New York, 4 October 2002.

Emceed by the television personality Karen Stone, the event was opened by Brigadier General Wilma Vaught, USAF Retired. Honorees received their medallions from Marilyn Bero, the President of the National Women's Hall of Fame, and the hall resounded with whistles, whoops, and cheers for each recipient. A standing ovation followed the spirited keynote speaker, Dr. Antonia C. Novello, the first woman and the first Latino to become the Surgeon General of the United States. The fiery Dr. Novello exhorted all to

continue the fight for equality for women; the "cause célèbre" that Emily championed in aviation.

Former United States Surgeon General Antonia Novello, keynote speaker at the 2001-2002 Induction of the National Women's Hall of Fame.

Displaying her keen wit, Dr. Novello said, "When I was Surgeon General of the United States, I learned many things. I learned that the world owes you nothing. To believe that the world is going to treat you [well] because you are a woman or a Surgeon General is like believing that a bull is not going to hit you because you're a vegetarian.

"...You would not be here if you did not feel that the lives of these women are worth celebrating. ... It is accepted that women can hold careers and hold jobs. ...I know that all of us who have gotten to the top have done so by sacrificing family, relationships, and personal time in favor of classes, meetings, and difficult assignments and, despite all the work that we have accomplished, we still receive only 75.7% of that received by men. ...I think the message should be clear. We women are not traditionally for charity, we are not succeeding because of political quotas. The time has come to promote women because we're good, not by favoritism of the majority.

"...It was only in 1920 that finally women got the right to vote. Today, 13 women are in the U.S. Senate; 62 women are in the House of Representatives, and there are 1662 women in state positions, 22% of all the legislators in this country. Who would have thought 150 years ago that 42% of medical school students would be women? 44% of law students would be women? Women outnumber the college enrollment of men by 1.5 million. The number of women as architects has nearly quadrupled. Women economists have nearly tripled. Women now comprise 50% of all journalists and 72% of all public relations firms in the U.S. are headed by women. ...Señores, we have arrived!

"...On top of that, when we get to the top, they say that we are 'lucky.' For me, taking advantage of opportunity, the more I work, the 'luckier' I seem to get. ...it seems to me that in spite of all the numbers..., the largest problem we have is gender bias. It continues to be the greatest deterrent to women. ...We need clear thinking and an absolute end to self-inflicted apathy and a real appreciation of the intellect, the training, and the accomplishments of women.

"...What we're asking for is equality and that is exactly what we need to do because in my mind many of the women's problems reflect the lack of empowerment of women in society, the lack of women in the planning culture, and the lack of accounting for societal problems that affect women throughout their lives. ...I say to you, what do we do now? ...First, in our local groups and in our own communities, make sure that we discover the needs, share the information, and combine our specialties so that we may be certain that we have the appropriations for that which we need. ...The country has to realize that without women this country will not go forward. ...there is no excuse for turning the human need and the claim of women into the hallowed theme of rhetoric or political gamesmanship. I think we should know better than that.

"More than anything, do not fall prey to complacency. ...Continually assess what you are doing and how well you are doing it. ... Let's hold management accountable for promoting women and for the advancement of women. Women have worked hard and should be able to step up the ladder equal to anybody else. ...more than anything, please make sure that women have the opportunity to take risks and ...have the choice to take on whatever they think is best for them. We all know that women have been slighted, sometimes consciously, sometimes unconsciously, at the workplace. Therefore, as women, do not deliver the sermon on equality. Live by it.

"…We cannot abdicate our course, we must absolutely advocate it. We need to tell our story on editorial pages, in every single magazine, every single television news channel, and in every political gathering because we as a group cannot establish our will if we are going to continue this great adventure. We cannot deprive the next generation of the opportunity to contribute. More than anything, we cannot afford to fail to engage in the very activities that will provide for the future the quality of life for women and for the movement of the agenda. But, as we listen to each one of us here today and we go home tomorrow, remember, when solutions come our way, we can no longer afford to sit back. We must watch the goal and have the persistence to keep looking for the outcome.

"…Martin Luther King used to say, 'When you are in doubt, ask yourself three questions. The first one is 'vanity.' Ask, 'would it look good?' 'Attitude,' ask, 'Would it work?' and 'Morality,' ask, 'Is it the right thing to do?' …You who have stood with the Great Women of the Hall of Fame, don't ever say that you stood as a bystander. Thank you very much and God Bless."

Television personality Karen Stone emceed the ceremony at the National Women's Hall of Fame.

With Emily's induction into the National Women's Hall of Fame, she became one of only nine women involved in aviation to be so honored to date. Named in the past were: Jacqueline Cochran, Eileen Collins, Amelia Earhart, Mae Jemison, Anne Morrow Lindbergh, Shannon Lucid, and Sally Ride. Inducted with Emily in 2002 was the late Bessie Coleman, the world's first African-American, man or woman, to be licensed as a pilot by the Fédération Aéronautique Internationale, whose aviation career ended in her premature accidental death in 1926. Accepting on behalf of Coleman was Willye White, a star athlete, who had been a member of 39 international teams, four Pan-American teams, and is the only American to compete—in the long jump, hurdles, and relays—on five consecutive U.S. Olympic track and field teams. In 1991, like Emily, eager to mentor young women in need of heroines for inspiration, she started the Willye White Foundation to assist young women in their life choices.

Bessie Coleman, the first U.S. black—man and woman—to become a licensed pilot, shown here in a portrait from the research archives of the Smithsonian's National Air & Space Museum, joined Emily as they became the seventh and eighth women inducted in the National Women's Hall of Fame whose achievements were in aviation. Her place of honor was accepted by the outstanding Olympic athlete, Willye White.

Why Seneca Falls, New York? One hundred and twenty five years before Emily Howell Warner was hired in 1973, Elizabeth Cady Stanton, a resident of Seneca Falls, instigated the Women's Rights Convention of 1848. Acting against the prevailing cultural mores that placed women as unequal to men in the eyes of the law, the church, or the government, she presented her Declaration of Sentiments, based on the U.S. Declaration of Independence, at that venue. At the time, women did not attend college, earn a living, hold elective office, or vote. The Convention of 1848 thrust her small town in the heart of the Finger Lakes Region of upstate New York into the limelight and brought to wide attention the necessity for women to be treated as equal citizens of the United States. Here, celebrating women's contributions to our nation, the National Women's Hall of Fame has existed since 1969.

The current President of the Board of Directors, Marilyn P. Bero, stated at the recent induction, 4-5 October 2002, "We are proud to honor these remarkable women whose achievements span centuries of American history. Their wisdom, determination, and bravery are of special significance this year, when stories of triumph and perseverance are needed more than ever. All of America should know about these women, be proud of these women, and use these great stories as a catalyst for renewed dedication and inspiration."

Brigadier General Wilma Vaught opened the ceremonies. The inductees were arranged alphabetically: Rosalynn Carter was seated second from the left, Barbara Holdridge was sixth from the left, and Emily Warner was the final inductee, seated at the extreme right. In front of the dais were Marilyn Bero, President, Board of Directors NWHOF, and Karen Stone, the mistress of ceremonies.

Of nineteen inductees, Emily Warner was one of four, with Rosalynn Carter, Ruth Bader Ginsburg, and Barbara Holdridge, who accepted the medal and the honor in person. Former First Lady Rosalynn Carter served as honorary chair of the Presidential Commission on Mental Health and founded "Every Child by Two," a successful immunization initiative. U.S. Supreme Court Justice Ginsburg is the second woman to sit on the federal bench and Holdridge is the creative co-founder, in 1952, of Caedmon Records, a woman-owned business that pioneered the concept of oral literary recordings featuring great writers and outstanding actors of the 20th century—the foundation for the audio books industry. Althea Gibson, tennis great, was too ill to appear and was represented by Fran Gray, the Executive Director of the Althea Gibson Foundation.

Ilene Yokoyama-Reed, with Emily at the induction ceremony, was instrumental with William and Penny Hamilton and Jay Warner in nominating Emily for this honor. Ilene said, "The achievements of Emily Warner have enduring value because what she did is unique. It cannot be repeated by anyone else. She cannot be replaced in her historic role. Moreover, her achievements set in motion a movement within the airline industry – the hiring of women co-pilots, pilots, and captains."

Thirteen of the awards were presented posthumously to the following list of auspicious women and their fields of endeavor: Dorothy Andersen, medicine; Lucille Ball, entertainment; Lydia Child, social activism; Paulina Davis, education; Dorothy Day, social justice; Marian de Forest, the founder of Zonta, a Service Organization; Katharine Graham, publishing; Beatrice Hicks, engineering; Bertha Holt, adoption children's services; Mary Pennington, chemistry and food preservation; Harriet Strong, dry land irrigation and water conservation; Mercy Otis Warren, poetry and drama; and Victoria Woodhull, the first woman to address Congress and the first to run for the office of the President of the United States. It was indeed gratifying and appropriate for Emily, who has represented aviation so well, to have been honored among the women who have shaped our nation and, indeed, our world.

Former First Lady Rosalynn Smith Carter, who has been an advocate for mental health, early childhood immunizations, human rights, conflict resolution, and health promotion, said, in her acceptance speech, "...I am honored to be at this place at this time. The place is significant, of course, because it is the birthplace of women's rights. And for me the timing could not be more meaningful. Beginning this week at the Carter Presidential Library, we have an exhibit called 'American Originals.' It includes the original Emancipation Proclamation, and, among other things, the arrest warrant of Susan B. Anthony when she attempted to vote in 1872.

Rosalynn Smith Carter, the former First Lady of the United States

"One of our first exhibits was... 'Women In The Constitution." We had about 2,000 people gathered to recognize women who played important roles in shaping the Constitution. Included were more than 150 of our first outstanding women leaders as well as many of the best known women leaders of today. ...The exhibition was an eye-opening experience for all of us as participants. We were startled by the significant role that women played. ...There is reason for great hope for ultimate equality for women. ...I am constantly in contact with young women who see no limitations for themselves. They cannot even imagine what it is like to be raised thinking they were not able to do something just because they were females. That's a good step in the right direction. Women in our country have always made great achievements, although they too often have gone unknown and unrecognized. The Women's Hall of Fame is the preeminent social force for publicizing their accomplishments and honoring these women. ..."

Justice Ruth Ginsburg noted, "...A student asked me, 'What did I think is the largest problem as we enter the coming century?' ...I thought of the Constitutional concept, 'We, the people ...' I thought ultimately of the United States and its motto, E Pluribus Unum—of many, one. That is the main aspiration. Understand, accommodate, even celebrate our differences while pulling together for the common good. 'Of many, one.' [That] is my hope for our nation and world..."

U.S. Supreme Court Justice Ruth Ginsburg receives her medal of induction into the National Women's Hall of Fame from Hall of Fame Board of Directors' President Marilyn Bero.

Toward the end of an inspirational and celebratory ceremony, Emily Hanrahan Howell Warner was the final honoree. Just prior to her introduction, Willye White had stated, "Bessie Coleman left a legacy for all women and people of color in aviation. If Bessie was here today, she would be delighted to share this day with Emily Howell Warner."

173

Karen Stone read, "Emily Howell Warner, you also fell in love with flying when you were young. You heard about a Norwegian woman who was hired to fly for SAS and set your sights on the same goal. Over the next 15 years, you amassed 7,000 flight hours, numerous FAA ratings and certificates: Private Pilot, Commercial, Instrument, Multi-engine, Instructor, and then Airline Transport Pilot. You were a flight instructor from 1961 until 1967 and by 1972, a Chief Pilot, Air Taxi and Flight School Manager, FAA Pilot and Examiner, and in charge of the United Air Lines contract training program for Clinton Aviation. You persevered through years of training male students who went on to pilot for various airlines. You then applied for an airline pilot position with Frontier Airlines. You came through a grueling simulator test and, in January 1973, were offered your dream opportunity. You made aviation history almost every time you boarded an airliner. You were the first female pilot for a scheduled U. S. passenger carrier; the first female captain; first to command the first all-female flight crew in the United States, and you were the first woman member of the Air Line Pilots Association (ALPA). You pioneered for today's more than 12,000 women piloting scheduled U.S. passenger flights. Your message to the next generation is that determination and persistence lead to success. For your extraordinary achievement in aviation and for advancing women's equality in aviation, you are inducted into the National Women's Hall of Fame. Please welcome Emily Howell Warner."

More than thirty of Emily's family and friends who had gathered from across the nation to share in her special moment leaped to their feet, clapping

and cheering. This was the acme of success; she was receiving deserved recognition of all of the years that she expended on behalf of aviation and on behalf of women. She took to the podium with the characteristic wit and poise for which she is known.

Emily accepts her honor.

"Is that applause because I am the final speaker?" she asked with a smile.

Then she continued, "I'm really, really proud and honored to be here today. I thank you, the National Women's Hall of Fame."

She turned to the tables that held her husband, Jay, and her family and friends, and said, "Thank you so much for coming."

"I'll just make a few remarks. When I found out at age eighteen that a woman can learn to fly in an airplane, I started taking flying lessons. I had wanted to be a stewardess, but after I started taking flying lessons, I changed my mind. By 1961, I had my flight instructor rating and was teaching mostly male pilots how to fly – and quite a few women, too.

"Two significant things happened in the Sixties that put ideas into my mind that started to work. One of them was the Civil Rights Movement and the other was the Women's Liberation Movement. A lot of other things were being debated in the United States as well – discrimination against age, gender, everything along those lines. I started to think that maybe a woman could be an airline pilot so I chose three airlines – United Air Lines, Continental, and old Frontier Airlines – Frontier was my favorite because I'd had my first airplane ride in a Frontier airliner – a DC-3. I started making applications in 1967 and it took me until 1973 to get a formal interview, finally, with Frontier Airlines. I was hired in January 1973.

"I thought that a woman at some point would be hired by an airline and as I got closer to 1973, things were started to hum in the airline industry and I knew that a lot of other women were kind of working toward that goal. I was 33 and I thought that I was perhaps too old, but remember, you couldn't discriminate on age either. My timing was perfect to go forward with this.

"I thought of people like Amelia Earhart, the Women Airforce Service Pilots, those who flew every available U.S. military aircraft during WWII and who were mentors for me. I met many of those women and they encouraged me with my own career. I also had many men who were peers and who encouraged my career. I want to thank every one of them. I hope that as I continue in my career that I can continue mentoring young people, especially women, in the aviation field.

"I just want to correct one of the statistics that was read. Actually, I just retired in June after 42 years in aviation. When I was hired, I happened to be the first. But now there are over 12,000 women pilots in the United States and there are about 100,000 male pilots with the airlines. So, with all the stats that were flying around earlier, it is only about 10% that are women. But, we've come a long way. United Air Lines has 2,500 woman pilots and about 350 of them are captains already. They are moving right up.

"Again, I'd like to thank the Hall Of Fame for this wonderful honor. ...It makes me think of a quote that I heard one time. This can apply to all of us. Think about this: 'We are all but grains of sand on the beach of eternity.' Thank you."

Grains of Sand

It was fitting that Emily stood with the "Great Women" of our nation. Her sentiments are echoed by the speakers whom attendees were privileged to hear. Her ideas are shared by those who count themselves as achievers and recognize their responsibility to contribute. She was pleased to receive a congratulatory card on her induction as well as on her retirement from Bonnie Tiburzi.

When the Education Office of the National Aeronautics and Space Administration developed a poster that encouraged young women to pursue careers in math, science, engineering, and technology and highlighted forty women "for remarkable achievements in aerospace in the 20th Century," Emily was included. Teresa M. Hudkins, the women's outreach manager for NASA Headquarters wrote, "Congratulations on your achievements, and thank you for being a role model for thousands of young women."

She added, "NASA has partnered with Women In Aviation International to conduct a nationwide program to interest young women in aerospace careers."

Emily responded to Teresa Hudkins, writing, "...I am very interested in continuing my interest and endeavors in the aviation field. I am especially interested in encouraging young women in aviation careers. I think the program, 'Consider a Career in Aerospace' would be right down my alley."

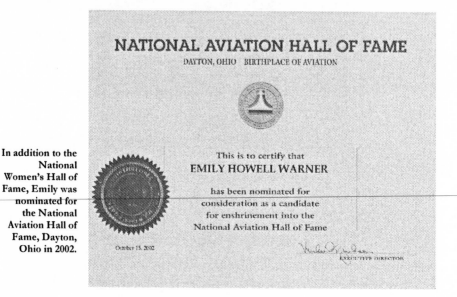

NATIONAL AVIATION HALL OF FAME
DAYTON, OHIO   BIRTHPLACE OF AVIATION

In addition to the National Women's Hall of Fame, Emily was nominated for the National Aviation Hall of Fame, Dayton, Ohio in 2002.

This is to certify that
EMILY HOWELL WARNER
has been nominated for consideration as a candidate for enshrinement into the National Aviation Hall of Fame

October 15, 2002

EXECUTIVE DIRECTOR

Emily was the keynote speaker at a Women In Aviation International Conference luncheon at which she said, "In 1934, Helen Richey was hired to fly an airliner, but she wasn't accepted by the male pilots. It took 39 years before they hired me. If there is one thing that is important to me, it is to encourage young women in their endeavors. I want them to pursue their dreams of becoming pilots with the nation's airlines. It is a great career field and I'd like to encourage women to set their goals high. We are just grains of sand now, but each one of us can help to build the beach."

If she had her life to live all over again, would she make some changes? Every modern woman who has made great achievements has made the sacrifices mentioned by Dr. Novello, who said, "...all of us who have gotten to the top have done so by sacrificing family, relationships, and personal time..." and every one harbors some regret. Emily would say that the person who is without regret is the person who has not reached beyond every boundary and every obstacle, the person who has not reached for the stars. As one who has known both regret and triumph, a Great Woman among Great Women, Emily stands on her achievements and turns to extend a hand to others who might choose to follow her into the sky. She knows from experience that she has woven the winds of chance, change, and opportunity into a fabulous career. She stands ready to fan those same winds into rising orbits of opportunity for countless young women. Come follow her into her beloved sky.

Portrait by Konrad Hack, ASAA

180

POSTLUDE: HIGHLIGHTS OF EMILY WARNER'S CAREER:

1967	Became Chief Pilot, Clinton Aviation, Denver, Colorado
1968	First Colorado woman to be appointed as a FAA Pilot Examiner
1972	First Member of the Colorado Pilots Association
1973	First Woman Pilot to be hired by a Scheduled, Jet-equipped Airline
1973	Colorado Wright Brothers Memorial Award for aviation contributions
1974	First Woman Pilot to become a member of ALPA
1976	First Woman to fly as a scheduled U.S. Airline Captain
1976	First Woman airline pilot to have her uniform enshrined in the Smithsonian National Air & Space Museum, Washington, DC
1978	A Charter Member of ISA +21
1981	Named to Captain's Club, ISA +21
1983	Inducted, Colorado Aviation Historical Society Hall of Fame
1983	Amelia Earhart Woman of the Year
1986	Hired by Continental Air Lines
1987	ISA +21 Honored Original 21 Charter Members
1988	Hired as Captain, United Parcel Service
1990	A Founding Member of the Friends of Granby Airport, Inc.
1990	Hired by Federal Aviation Administration, Air Carrier Inspector
1991	Inducted, International Forest of Friendship
1992	Inducted, Women In Aviation International Pioneer Women Hall of Fame
1992	The Captain Warner Aviation Education Resource Center established by the Friends of Granby Airport, Inc.
1993	Colorado General Assembly passed Resolution 94-29 honoring Captain Warner for her historic role in American Aviation History
1994	Salute to Women Award, FAA Western Pacific Region, Federal Women's Program Committee
2000	Opening of the Captain Emily Hanrahan Howell Warner Permanent Display, Wings Over the Rockies Air and Space Museum, created by: Friends of Granby Airport, Colorado Aviation Historical Society, Colorado Pilots Association, Wings Over the Rockies Air and Space Museum, Rocky Mountain Aviation and Aerospace Association, and Frontier Airlines.
2000	Inducted, Colorado Women's Hall of Fame
2001	Emily Howell Warner Day proclaimed on 26 November by Colorado Governor, Bill Owens
2002	Inducted, National Women's Hall of Fame
2002	Nominated, National Aviation Hall of Fame

BIBLIOGRAPHY: WEAVING THE WINDS, Emily Warner

Allen, Oliver E. and the Editors, Time-Life Books. *THE AIRLINE BUILDERS*, Time-Life Books, Alexandria, VA, 1981.

Bilstein, Roger E. *FLIGHT IN AMERICA*, 1900-1983, The Johns Hopkins University Press, Baltimore and London, 1984.

Brooks-Pazmany, Kathleen. *United States Women in Aviation 1919-1929*, Smithsonian Institution Press, Washington, 1983.

Carl, Ann Baumgartner; speech at dedication of Dorothy Swain Lewis memorial statue to the WASP, U.S. Air Force Museum, Dayton, Ohio, 1993.

Christy, Joe. *HIGH ADVENTURE, The First 75 Years of Civil Aviation*, TAB Books, Inc., Blue Ridge Summit, Pennsylvania, 1985.

Cooper, Charlie and Cooper, Ann. *Tuskegee's Heroes, as featured in the Aviation Art of Roy E. La Grone.* Motorbooks International, Osceola, Wisconsin, 1996.

Davies, R.E.G., *AIRLINES OF THE UNITED STATES SINCE 1914*, Smithsonian Institution Press, Washington, DC, 1998. First published in Great Britain in 1972.

Davies, R.E.G., *FALLACIES AND FANTASIES OF AIR TRANSPORT HISTORY*, Paladwr Press, McLean, Virginia, 1994.

Douglas, Deborah. *United States Women in Aviation 1940-1985*, Smithsonian Institution Press, Washington and London, 1991.

Granger, Byrd Howell; *ON FINAL APPROACH, The Women Airforce Service Pilots of World War II*, Falconer Publishing Company, Scottsdale, Arizona, 1991.

Heppenheimer, T.A., *TURBULENT SKIES*, John Wiley & Sons, Inc., New York, 1995.

Holden, Henry and Griffith, Lori; *LADYBIRDS II, The Continuing Story of Women Pilots in America.* Black Hawk Publishing Company, New Jersey, 1993.

Hopkins, George E. *FLYING THE LINE, The First Half Century of the Air Line Pilots Association*, The Air Line Pilots Association, Washington, DC, 1982.

Imeson, Sparky. *MOUNTAIN FLYING*, Airguide Publications, Inc., Long Beach, CA, 1987.

Jane's *Encyclopedia of Aviation*, Compiled and Edited by Michael J.H. Taylor, Bestseller Publications, Ltd., London, originally published in 1980, updated in 1989.

Kerfoot, Glenn. *PROPELLER ANNIE, The Story of Helen Richey*, Kentucky Aviation History Roundtable, Lexington, KY, 1988.

Kimball, Roger. *The Long March, How The Cultural Revolution of the 1960s Changed America*, Encounter Books, San Francisco, 2000.

Marwick, Arthur. *The Sixties: Cultural Revolution in Britain, France, Italy, and the United States, c. 1958-1974*, Oxford University Press, 1998.

McGuire, Jerry and Warner, Emily Howell. *LEARNING HOW TO FLY AN AIRPLANE*, TAB Books, Blue Ridge Summit, PA.

Moolman, Valerie and the Editors, Time-Life Books. *WOMEN ALOFT*, Time-Life Books, Alexandria, VA, 1981.

Morrison, Steven A. and Winston, Clifford. *THE EVOLUTION OF THE AIRLINE INDUSTRY*, The Brookings Institution, Washington, DC, 1995.

Murphy, Daryl E. *THE AVIATION FACT BOOK*, McGraw-Hill, New York, 1998.

Nichols, Ruth. *WINGS FOR LIFE*, J.B. Lippincott Company, Philadelphia and New York, 1957.

Norris, Captain Bob and Mortensen, Danny. *THE AIRLINE CAREER AND INTERVIEW MANUAL*, Aviation Business Services, Rancho Cordova, California, 1991.

Oakes, Claudia. *United States Women in Aviation through World War I*, Smithsonian Institution Press, Washington, 1978.

Oakes, Claudia. *United States Women in Aviation 1930-1939*, Smithsonian Institution Press, Washington, 1985.

Otypka, Sylvia J. *FLYING THE BIG BIRDS, On Becoming An Airline Pilot*, Leading Edge Publishing, Aurora, CO, 1997.

Peterson, Barbara Sturken and Glab, James. *RAPID DESCENT, Deregulation and the Shakeout In The Airlines*, Simon and Shuster, Inc., New York, 1994.

Petzinger, Thomas, Junior. *HARD LANDING, The Epic Contest for Power and Profits that Plunged the Airlines into Chaos*, Random House, Inc., New York, 1995.

Planck, Charles E. *WOMEN WITH WINGS*, Harper and Brothers, New York and London, 1942.

Searle, Tex. *THE GOLDEN YEARS OF FLYING*, Mountain Empire Publishing Company, Orem, Utah, 1998.

Serling, Robert J. *SHE'LL NEVER GET OFF THE GROUND*, Doubleday & Company, Inc., Garden City, New York, 1971.

Saint Exupéry, Antoine de. *WIND, SAND, AND STARS*, Lewis Galantiere, translator. HBJ Modern Classic, Harcourt Brace, New York, Reissued October, 1992.

Tanner, Doris Brinker. *WHO WERE THE WASP?*, a compilation of newspaper articles from *Fifinella Gazette* and *The Avenger* and dated between 1942 and 1944, 1989.

Taylor, Michael J.H., Editor, *JANE'S ENCYCLOPEDIA OF AVIATION*, Portland House, New York, 1989. Originally published in London, 1980.

Tiburzi, Bonnie and Moolman, Valerie. *TAKEOFF!* "An Eleanor Friede Book," Crown Publishers, Inc., New York, New York, 1984.

Titterington, Diane, Producer. *SPEAKING OF FLYING*, The Aviation Speakers Bureau, San Clemente, CA, 2000.

The Boeing Company. *PEDIGREE OF CHAMPIONS, Boeing Since 1916*. May 1985.

Unger, Irwin and Unger, Debi, Editors. *the times were a-changin'- the sixties reader*, Three Rivers Press, New York, 1998.

Reference Books:

Encarta®98 Desk Encyclopedia©, 1996-97 Microsoft Corporation.

The American Heritage Dictionary of the English Language, Houghton Mifflin Company, 1996.

The World Almanac® and Book of Facts 1997, K-III Reference Corporation, 1996.

Magazine, Newspaper, and Internet Articles:

Airline Handbook, Copyright 2000, Air Transport Association of America, Inc. *ata@air-transport.org*

Grey, George. "Multi-culturalism Threat Looms," *The Spectrum Daily News*, St. George, Utah, Vol. 35, No. 5, 4 March 2001.

Hamilton, Penny; "Nation's First Lives Here," *Winter Park Manifest*, Winter Park, Colorado; page 14.

Hamilton, Penny and Hamilton, William. "On The Wings Of Dreams, Colorado Woman Takes Flight," *Colorado Country Life*, Colorado Rural Electric Association, March 2001.

History of Flight, "Celebrating The Evolution of Flight, 1903-2003 ...and Beyond," American Institute of Aeronautics and Astronautics, Reston, Virginia, 2001. http://www.flight100.org/history

Horowitz, Daniel. "Rethinking Betty Friedan and *The Feminine Mystique:* Labor Union Radicalism and Feminism in Cold War America, *American Quarterly*, The American Studies Association, 48.1, 1996.

Kellner, Douglas. *Herbert Marcuse*, Internet, 2000.

LeDuff, Charlie. "Perry H. Young Jr. , Pioneering Pilot," *New York Times*, 19 November 1998.

Longman, Jere. "The Untold Story of Flight 93," from Among the Heroes: the Story of Flight 93, *Reader's Digest*, September 2002.

The American Heritage® Dictionary of the English Language, Third Edition © 1996 by Houghton Mifflin Company. Electronic version licensed from INSO Corporation; further reproduction and distribution in accordance with the Copyright Law of the United States.

Nolly, George. "The Road To Victory: My First Airline Interview," *The AVweb Group*, 2000.

Nolte, Eric. "The Government Spiral," *AirlineSafety.com*, 2000.

Oden, Wendy; "Captain Emily Warner: An Inspiration In Aviation," *The Stapleton InnerLine*, Wood Publications, Inc., Aurora, Colorado, 29 September 1994, pages 6-7.

Patterson, James T. "John Fitzgerald Kennedy" and "Lyndon Baines Johnson," biographies, *Grolier Incorporated 2000*, Internet.

Rosen, Elliot A. *Grolier Encyclopedia 2000*, Internet

Ross, Lance. "Groundbreaking Pilot Emily Warner to Keynote Aurora Library Series," *The Stapleton InnerLine*, Wood Publications, Inc., Aurora, Colorado, 1 September 1994, pages 12, 15.

Satchell, Michael. "Now Women Pilots Get Their Turn With The Airlines," *PARADE, The Sunday Newspaper Magazine*, New York, 25 June 1978, p. 6-7.

http://www.avstop.com/history

http://inmemoriamonline.net/Profiles

http://facweb.stvincent.edu/academics/english/faculty/wissolik/ritchey.htm

http://www.iswap.org/richey.html

http://www.airodyssey.net/articles/movie-flt232.html

http://www.airdisaster.com/photos/ua232/photo.shtml

INDEX

About the Author:

Believing that "Amelia Earhart wasn't the only woman pilot," Ann Lewis Cooper, a flight instructor and aviation author, has proved it. Having published the stories of four women pilots who made aviation history: Edna Gardner Whyte (*RISING ABOVE IT*), Jessie Woods (*ON THE WING*), Dot Swain Lewis (*HOW HIGH SHE FLIES*), and Patty Wagstaff (*FIRE and AIR*), she now offers *WEAVING THE WINDS, Emily Howell Warner.* With her husband Charlie, Cooper has co-authored *TUSKEGEE'S HEROES, HOW TO DRAW AIRCRAFT LIKE A PRO,* and *WAR IN PACIFIC SKIES.* Cooper edited *AERO BRUSH,* the newsletter of the American Society of Aviation Artists for 12 years. Her freelance articles have been published in *Sport Aviation, Sport Pilot, Kitplanes, Private Pilot,* and *Aviation History.*

Printed in the United States
16071LVS00003B/79-267